8   *THE CONCEPTUALISATION OF EUROPE*   Barbara Steiner
12   *A WELCOME FROM THE GOETHE-INSTITUT*   Johannes Ebert
14   *EUROPE^n FESTIVAL*
23   *ABOUT THE BEGINNING*   Sabine Hentzsch, Ilina Koralova

35   *SPECULATION AND IMPLEMENTATION*   Barbara Steiner

75   *EUROPE, THE EUROPEAN UNION, AND ART*   Tone Hansen, Filip Luyckx, Peio Aguirre, Jun Yang, Kit Hammonds, Miško Šuvaković, Esra Sarigedik Öktem, Lena Prents, Jarosław Lubiak, Joanna Sokołowska

89   *CARRYING EUROPE AROUND*   Barbara Steiner
91   *EXCHANGING SCENARIOS – EXCHANGING IDEAS*   Kit Hammonds, Filip Luyckx, Lena Prents, Jarosław Lubiak, Joanna Sokołowska, Miško Šuvaković, Peio Aguirre, Tone Hansen, Esra Sarigedik Öktem, Jun Yang

115   *SINGLE AND COMMON AGENDAS*   Barbara Steiner
117   *A CURRENCY OF CONTENTION*   Oliver Klimpel

149   *ADVERTISING EUROPE THROUGH FILM*   Florian Wüst
163   *A EUROPEAN EXHIBITION SPACE*   Christian Teckert

185   *COLLECTIVE COMMUNICATION AND THE EUROPE^n CLOUD*   Christopher Köhler
191   *A PORTRAIT OF SPECIFIC INTERESTS AND AGENDAS*   Oliver Klimpel, Christian Teckert
195   *SHARED RESPONSIBILITY*   Kit Hammonds, Lena Prents, Joanna Sokołowska, Jarosław Lubiak, Lara Fresko, Esra Sarigedik Öktem, Tone Hansen, Miško Šuvaković, Filip Luyckx, Peio Aguirre, Jun Yang

209   *ABOUT THE FORMATION OF EUROPE^n*   Sabine Hentzsch, Ilina Koralova, Barbara Steiner
215   *THE MAKING OF EUROPE^n*   Barbara Steiner
227   Biographies of Artists and Participants, Colophon

A project with an emphasis on a multilayered and multiple Europe expressed in the mathematical notation *Europe (to the power of) n,* indicating there is not one Europe but many – interconnected and overlapping.

The Europe^n-Book

OSLO

LONDON

BRUSSELS

DONOSTIA–
SAN SEBASTIÁN

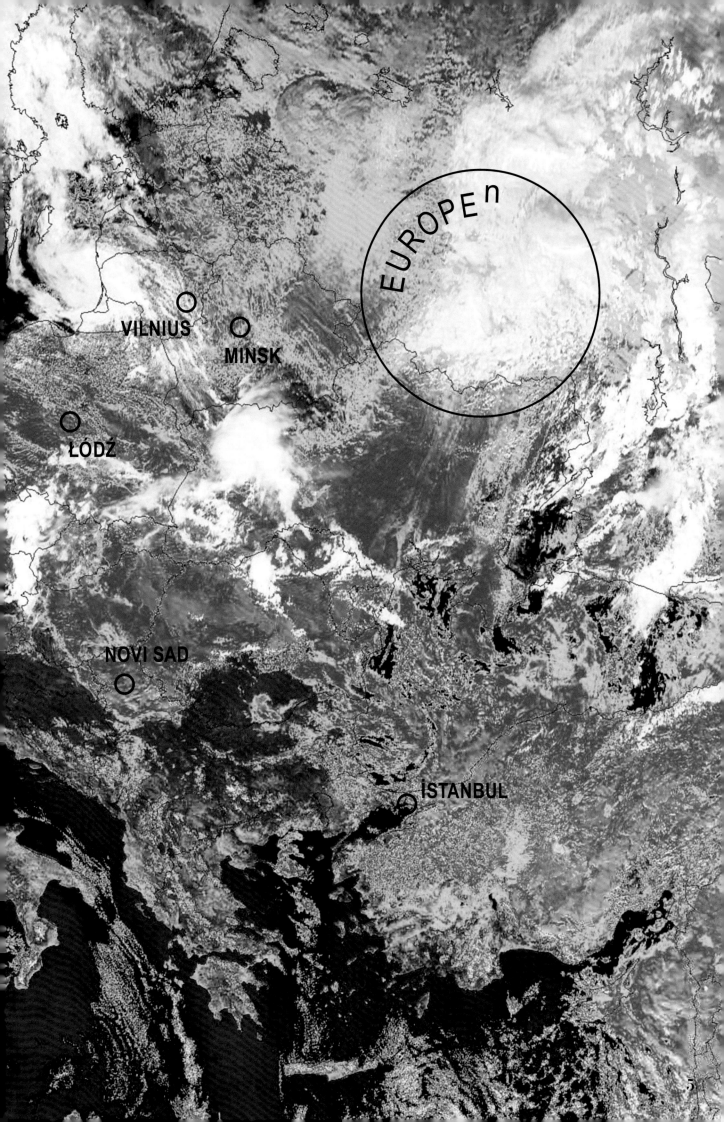

EUROPEn

VILNIUS

MINSK

ŁÓDŹ

NOVI SAD

İSTANBUL

5

Michaël Aerts, Akademia Ruchu, Reza Aramesh,
Sven Augustijnen, Davide Bertocchi, Boris Bezić,
Mohamed Bourouissa, Gast Bouschet & Nadine Hilbert,
Jérémie Boyard, Olaf Breuning, Veronica Brovall,
Jovan Čekić, Banu Cennetoğlu, Jeannette Christensen,
Clegg & Guttmann, Zorica Čolić, Joost Conijn, Tim Eitel,
Köken Ergun, Annika Eriksson, Priscila Fernandes,
Harrell Fletcher / Ella Aandal, Sylvie Fleury, Peter Friedl,
Rainer Ganahl, Iñaki Garmendia, Stephan Geene,
Johan Van Geluwe, Melanie Gilligan, Florian Göthner,
goldiechiari, Goldin+Senneby, Dejan Grba, Group ABS,
Živko Grozdanić, Ane Hjort Guttu, Jens Haaning,
Lise Harlev, Eberhard Havekost, IRWIN, Asako Iwama,
Luis Jacob, Janez Janša, Janez Janša, Janez Janša,
Isaac Julien, Agnieszka Kalinowska, Abbas Kiarostami,
Oliver Klimpel, Servet Koçyiğit, Aleksander Komarov,
KwieKulik, Darcy Lange, Andrei Liankevich,
Anikó Lóránt & Tamás Kaszás, Erik Løchen, Line Løkken,
Marisol Malatesta, Carin Mannheimer, Enrique Marty,
Tony Matelli, Josephine Meckseper, Asier Mendizabal,
Philip Metten, Jonathan Monk, Nástio Mosquito,
Edvard Munch, Marina Naprushkina, Palle Nielsen,
Frank Nitsche, Nils Norman, Øystein Wyller Odden,
Ahmet Öğüt, Wendelien van Oldenborgh, Tadej Pogačar,
Provisional SALTA Ensemble, Nika Radić,
Reynold Reynolds & Patrick Jolley, Stefan Rusu,

Xabier Salaberria, Diego Santomé, Ariel Schlesinger,
Hannes Schmid, Anne-Marie Schneider, Allan Sekula,
Sergey Shabohin, Jura Shust, Janek Simon,
Arvid Skauge / Nils Utsi, Slavs and Tatars,
Kjartan Slettemark, Nedko Solakov, Helmut Stallaerts,
Jean-Marie Straub / Danièle Huillet, Christian Teckert,
Nataša Teofilović, Peter Tillberg, Lincoln Tobier,
Zoran Todorović, Polona Tratnik, Dragomir Ugren,
Koen Vanmechelen, Mona Vătămanu & Florin Tudor,
Heidi Voet, Daniel James Wilkinson, Jun Yang,
Katarina Zdjelar, Hannes Zebedin

The project *Europe (to the power of) n* started with the a priori statement that a rigorous, unambiguous definition of Europe – be it geographically or culturally – is impossible. Taking into consideration that over the centuries Europe has had various shapes, that it has always been a congeries of people having very different roots and backgrounds, widely diverse ideas and attitudes, the project places emphasis on a multilayered and multiple Europe. This is last but not least expressed in the mathematical notation *Europe (to the power of) n*. In fact, there is not one

Europe, but many; they interconnect and overlap, they repel each other and come into conflict.

Europe (to the power of) n asks, what if we looked positively into Europe's condition described here and examined the possibilities involved. Could we imagine a Europe without a central authority, a Europe that gives space to disagreement and, nevertheless, finds ways of setting up a being-in-common? Yet, how to define our relationship to those who challenge an exclusive European community, who cause disturbance, and introduce different ideas and values? Even if the directive is "United in Diversity", as in the case of the European Union, when conferred upon the entire association this means a union that stands against another union, however varied it may be within itself. Today, nobody really can provide a formula for how to practically live in a society that is based on diversity and disagreement. But let us – at least for a moment – think differently about the possibilities Europe might have. Because of its diversity, which has grown more or less historically, because of its conflicts and contradictions, but also due to its traumatised past of wars and genocide, Europe could offer ideal conditions for conceiving a non-consensual society that gives space to disagreement and agreement, that opens up without getting lost, and that establishes mutual relationships to others. Both, to give space to in-congruent voices *and* to establish rela-tionships to those who are not in line with oneself, are exactly what the project *Europe (to the power of) n* tries to do on a miniature scale.

Barbara Steiner

A Welcome from the Goethe-Institut

The Goethe-Institut must, and indeed wishes, to take on the world's processes of transformation as a challenge. Faced with the changes occurring in the course of globalisation, questions are raised about how we conduct our work in, with, and about Europe. As our experiences of working together as one half of a partnership with the ninety-three host countries in which the Goethe-Institut is located form the basis of our work – our sights are never singularly directed towards our own continent. Rather, these communities are very much a part of the tensions that form the relationship between metropolises and spaces on the periphery, and the positioning of Europe in a multipolar world. These considerations were at the start of a process that led to our trans-regional project *Europe (to the power of) n*. Our goal was an unconventional European art project that would address the current questions on Europe by reflecting and commenting on them through artistic means, reaching far beyond the geographic borders of the continent. The initiation of this artistic process, the effectiveness of which remains open and is unfolding at this very moment, belongs to an approach chosen by Barbara Steiner, Artistic Director of the project, and her international curatorial team: they developed thirty scenarios from artistic and curatorial perspectives that reflect on the Europe of today. This polyphony shows a diverse Europe, but also its contradictions and crises. Between July 2012 and April 2013 the scenarios were introduced, contextualised, and extended upon in eleven locations within and outside of the European Union in collaboration with the local Goethe-Institutes, museums, universities, contemporary arts centres, as well as alternative arts spaces in Brussels, İstanbul, London, Łódź, Minsk, Vilnius, Novi Sad, Høvikodden near Oslo, Donostia – San Sebastián, Beijing, and Taipei.

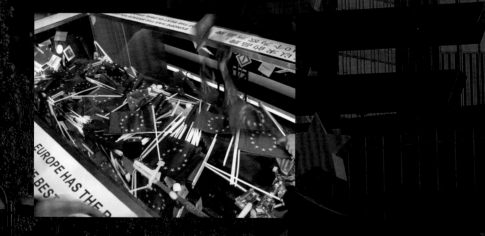

At this point, I would like to give my heartfelt thanks to Barbara Steiner, the curatorial team, and the entire project team, along with all partnering institutions involved for their hard work, creativity, and innovative approaches in achieving this European art project. I would also like to thank Sabine Hentzsch and the colleagues at all participating Goethe-Institutes who have made this project a success. I must also thank the European Commission's Culture Programme and the Robert Bosch Foundation as well as the Allianz Cultural Foundation and Dr. Arend Oetker.

Johannes Ebert, General Secretary of the Goethe-Institut

Berlin,
Europe^n-Festival

On 6 and 7 July, 2012, *Europe (to the power of) n* was launched at the Haus der Kulturen der Welt in Berlin. Within this frame, the project was introduced and a series of scenarios of how to think about Europe was presented to the audience. In equal measure, the festival offered an insight into the upcoming exhibitions at the various locations. The focus of the films, lectures, lecture-performances, performances, and talks was on a Europe that does not defend an exclusive identity but opens itself up, that sets itself in relation to others taking into consideration its colonial, non-European past, its current migrant imprints, and its increasing global interdependencies.

ASAKO IWAMA
Incorporation, 2012
Artist: Asako Iwama, Actor: Matthias Neukirch,
Camera: Joji Koyama and Montse Torreda
(installation views)

On the occasion of the *Europe^n-Festival*
at the Haus der Kulturen der Welt, Matthias Neukirch
was invited by Asako Iwama to perform her role.
The accompanying film, in which Neukirch is seen to be
mimicking Iwama's cooking of riceballs (a process in
which the hands of the maker become an integral tool),
documents the process of his "becoming" Iwama.

The Festival introduced to the project *Europe*^{n}. Films, lectures, lecture-performances, performances, and talks offered a wide range of approaches on how to think about Europe from the perspective of art.

Bernd M. Scherer, Director of Haus der Kulturen der Welt, welcomed speakers and audience.

Sabine Hentzsch, Co-initiator of *Europe*^{n} and Director of the Goethe-Institut in London

Oliver Klimpel, Designer, Visual Identity of *Europe*^{n}

Köken Ergun, Artist

Barbara Steiner, Artistic Director of *Europe*^{n}

Christian Teckert, Architect, Spatial Identity of *Europe*^{n}

Jarosław Lubiak and
Joanna Sokołowska,
Łódź Curators

Koen Vanmechelen, Artist

Janez Janša, Janez
Janša, Janez Janša,
Artists

Kit Hammonds,
London Curator

Lena Prents, Minsk
Curator, and Aleksander
Komarov, Artist

Filip Luyckx,
Brussels Curator

Peio Aguirre, Donostia –
San Sebastián Curator,
and Annika Eriksson,
Artist

Slavs and Tatars,
Artist Group

Miško Šuvaković,
Novi Sad Curator

Jun Yang, Beijing and
Taipei Curator

Tone Hansen,
Høvikodden / Oslo
Curator

EUROPEⁿ

Europeⁿ
Festival

...turen

...2012

...tag, 06. Juli 2012

...ch
...glischer Übersetzung

...Uhr
...de

...n W...
...ma...
...äser...

...eten
...blik
...e Ge...
...o ger...
...tein
...ne E...
...et in ihrem im Wochenschaustil
...Dokumentarfilm über die
...und die Ziele der Montanunion
...edeutung von Kohle und Stahl für
...e Leben.

...nung sprechen:
...nerer, Intendant Haus der
...der Welt;
...Ebert, Generalsekretär
...nstitut

...rs, 5 min,
...öthner

...von *Neighbours* spielt mit den
...n Nähe und Distanz. Die real
...Landschaftscollagen sind
...er", virtuelle Räume, mit offenen
...n und Verbindungen.

...r, Vortrag:
...n Kunstprojekt über Europa
..., Barbara Steiner

...*Europeⁿ* versucht eine Annäh-
...n Europa, das pluralistisch, hetero-
...und in sich widersprüchlich ist.
...beschreibt die Schwierigkeiten und
...eines solchen Kunstprojekts, und
...ennoch nach wie vor interessant
..., über Europa zu sprechen.

...r, Vortrag:
...h und Feindlich.
...dentitäten im Projekt
...Oliver Klimpel

S...

P...
in...

...exities?
...a Boni, Andreja
...chulze mit
...Wissenschaft,

..., Andreja
...e haben eine
...ntwickelt, die
...n, Vermittlung
und Kommunikation von *Europeⁿ* dient.
Dabei werden dynamische und kontinuierlich
erweiterbare Verbindungen zwischen Themen,
Konzepten, Orten und Menschen hergestellt.
Im Workshop soll das Potenzial dieses im
Kulturbereich entwickelten Projekts für andere
gesellschaftliche Bereiche ausgelotet werden.

12.00 Uhr   Pause

13.00 Uhr, Film:
Binibining Promised Land, Köken
Ergun, 2009, 30 min

Köken Erguns Film adressiert die Situation der
philippinischen Gastarbeiterinnen in Israel und
zeigt die Bindungskraft einer transnationalen
Gemeinschaft. Am Beispiel des bekanntesten
Schönheitswettbewerbs der Filipinas in Tel Aviv
spricht er von den Realitäten und Träumen
seiner ProtagonistInnen, davon wie sich die
Filipinas unter den neuen Lebensumständen
einrichten, ihre Traditionen fortsetzen und
auch neu schreiben. Der Film handelt von
Dislozierung und Verortung gleichermaßen
und auch davon, wie sehr Teile der Welt durch
Migration zusammengerückt sind.

13.45 Uhr, Vortragsperformance:
Genetic Freedom, Koen Vanmechelen

Der belgische Künstler Koen Vanmechelen
widmet sich biokultureller Diversität. Er stellt
sein *Cosmopolitan Chicken Project* vor,
in dem er die Genealogie des Huhns zum
Ausgangspunkt für seine künstlerischen
Arbeiten nimmt. Vanmechelen greift in den
Züchtungsprozess ein, indem er nationale
Züchtungen und die daraus resultierenden
Hybride mehrfach kreuzt.

..., und
...glichkeiten
...zudenken,
...ngspunkt
...s *Europeⁿ*,
...2012
...Brüssel,
...Łódź,
Minsk, Novi Sad, Høvikodden/
Oslo, San Sebastián und
Beijing als transregionales
Exzellenzprojekt des Goethe-
Instituts stattfindet. De...
Auftakt macht ein Fes...
Haus der Kulturen der...
in dessen Rahmen ein...
Auswahl an Szenarie...
deren Protagonisten v...
stellt werden.

Das dem Projekt zugr...
liegende Europa steht...
herausfordernden Bez...
ungen zu anderen und...
herausgefordert. Es ve...
digt nicht Identität und...
Einheit, sondern öffne...
Über die künstlerische...
Arbeiten wird Europa...
Beziehung zu anderer...
gesetzt, im Wissen um...
koloniale Vergangenhe...
seine gegenwärtige m...
tische Prägung und zur...
mende globale Verflechtungen.

Europa ist kein Solitär!

The *Europe*^{n}-Team on the staircase of the Haus der Kulturen der Welt, Berlin

The artist and cook Thomas Wrobel founded "Chinabrenner" in Leipzig in 2006. It is modelled after a small, shut down cook shop in Chengdu, where three elderly women cooked for their guests. To refresh and to deepen his knowledge, Wrobel makes periodic research trips to the province of Sichuan in the west of China. "Chinabrenner" was invited to cook for the guests of the festival in Berlin.

WELCHES EUROPA?
Europe^n Festival im Haus der Kulturen der Welt Berlin

6. 7. 2012, 18 – 24 Uhr
7. 7. 2012, 10 – 24 Uhr

Design: Oliver Klimpel

EUROPI^n
Festival

Vorträge / Filme / Performances von:
Peio Aguirre, Köken Ergun, Annika Eriksson, Melanie Gilligan, Florian Göthner, Kit Hammonds, Ane Hjort Guttu, Tone Hansen, Asako Iwama, Janez Janša, Janez Janša, Janez Janša, Oliver Klimpel, Aleksander Komarov, Eva Kroll, Jarosław Lubiak, Filip Luyckx, Lena Prents, Luise Schröder, Slavs and Tatars, Joanna Sokołowska, Barbara Steiner, Miško Šuvaković, Koen Vanmechelen, Thomas Wrobel, Florian Wüst, Jun Yang

EUROPEn

EUROPEⁿ
Festival

Diese
Veranstaltung
wird *gefilmt*.

Ilina Koralova:
How did the idea for the *Europe (to the power of) n* project develop?

Sabine Hentzsch:
The Goethe-Institut has been exploring the theme of Europe through both internal and external events for a long time. There are also regular meetings for intense internal brainstorming between the European regions where the Goethe-Institut is active to explore the question: how can we fully use the potential of our work not just for one country or one region, but in such a way that it overlaps all regions and deals with the question of Europe from an artistic perspective? When we were at one such brainstorming session four years ago, it became clear to us: we did not want to do a touring exhibition called something like "Images of Europe" or "European Art", but rather thematically define Europe. It should be an exhibition that would take place not in a single place, but in many different places across the regions while taking the local context seriously.

IK: And to consider the local context meant to involve the local partners – curators as well as institutions, not only the Goethe-Institutes in the respective locations?

SH: The partnerships were very important to us, because we did not want the Goethe-Institut to act as some kind of missionary arriving with a big exhibition and announcing "This is Europe". This would contradict our dialogical approach and our collaborative orientation.

IK: *Europe (to the power of) n* is taking place over a long period of time, which is unusual in general, but even

more so for the Goethe-Institut. Directors at the Goethe-Institutes change every few years. One of the project's initiators, Heiko Sievers, is no longer in Cairo for example.

SH: We are liable to rotation, which means that we are relocated every few years. But such a rotation would never work if decisions and agreements on projects made beforehand were not made binding. The Goethe-Institut is not that person-centric. But it is correct that Heiko Sievers was the first person who began to think about which possible themes within the context of Europe could be interesting. He wanted one more person from our circle to be involved and I was immediately intrigued.

IK: At the time you were in Bucharest, Rumania. Did this fact somehow influence the decision to support Heiko Sievers' idea?

SH: I was in Bucharest and then moved from Southeast Europe to London. Therefore, I got the chance to have both a Western and Eastern European perspective on the subject of Europe. As Director of the Goethe-Institut in Bucharest, I could follow Rumania's ascension into the EU; in London the question of Europe is more difficult than in other places. However, when Heiko left the European neighbourhood for India – I consider Cairo to be part of Europe – we had decided between us that I would take over. It was, after all, a regional project. You could put it like this: ideally we would work together, but the implementation would be lead from one place, in this case London.

IK: Over time, the project seemed to have developed new dynamics. The wish to work with partners in different places was difficult to manage due to their very diverse backgrounds.

SH: We would not be able – and in any case did not want – to realise this project on our own, so we looked for competent partners. We also looked for an Artistic Director for *Europe (to the power of) n*, and became acquainted with Barbara Steiner. We also could not finance this project on our own. In as many cases as possible we try to split the costs fifty-fifty with our partners, but it has been the case that not all of them are in the same economic circumstances that we are in. If both sides cannot cover the whole budget, we look for external financial aid. *Europe (to the power of) n* is complicated from every angle as we are working in completely different countries with different economies, but also with different institutions within these countries.

IK: Even in a country like Germany, the ability of an institution to cope with international projects and bigger budgets would vary from city to city. This applies especially to *Europe (to the power of) n*. Take art galleries in states such as Belarus as an example ...

SH: It makes a huge difference whether we are in cooperation with an established museum or with a small gallery that has to work under difficult political circumstances. They dictate completely different points of departure. The countries themselves also have their own attitudes, practices and regulations, which we cannot simply override. All this needs to be taken into account. This is why the splitting of the preparation and implementation phases was so important. The project needed a relatively long period of groundwork. Actually, it was always a "work-in-progress".

IK: Was time a factor in convincing the partner institutions, too?

SH: Although the Goethe-Institut has already been working with some of the partners in certain countries for a long time, the amount of time it required just to work out the contacts was enormous. We have been in contact with the Royal College of Art in London for many years. For SALT in İstanbul this was a further collaboration with the Goethe-Institut İstanbul. The Goethe-Institut in Poland has certainly supported previous projects in Łódź. But Poland is a big country, there are so many important cultural centres that Łódź has not been at the top of the list and the considerable work we did together with the Muzeum Sztuki was a new and very positive experience. Getting to know new partners with such positive results was the case in Novi Sad and Minsk.

IK: When we explain that *Europe (to the power of) n* is taking place in Novi Sad and in Łódź we are often asked "why isn't the project taking place in Warsaw?" and "why not in Belgrade?"

SH: It was, of course, a completely conscious decision within Barbara Steiner's conceptualisation to foreground the theme of periphery, even when discussing capital cities like Brussels or London. Periphery in this context means an acknowledged distance to a strongly unified Europe and the European Union. In the case of Brussels she has put forward a paradox – on the one hand Brussels is the capital of the EU, and on the other hand it is the capital of a country full of social tension. It became apparent that those cities, which are usually mentioned in the same breath as Europe – for example Paris – are not as important for our project. It was about throwing a spanner in the works of Europe, if you like. And this is why I regret that collaborations in Athens and Alexandria did not work out. Unfortunately, we could not convince the institutions to participate.

During the scenario period of the project, different perspectives about Europe were explored. They provided arguments for the visual identity of *Europe^n*.
Designs by Oliver Klimpel and Aurelia Markwalder

London

London's influence in politics, finance, education, entertainment, media, fashion, and the arts contributes to its leading global position and makes the city attractive to many people from all over the world. London hosts a diverse range of ethnic groups, cultures, and religions, and hundreds of languages are spoken within its boundaries. The United Kingdom's connection to the world, expressed in the vibrant atmosphere of its capital and its international policy – which enjoys good relations with the Arab World, India, and the US – is contrasted by its special way of sealing off when it comes to European agendas. Generally, the UK has always taken a defensive position in regards to further steps towards its integration into the European Union. In the past few years, the UK's policy towards the European Union has been nourished by considerations of leaving the EU. First and foremost, the economic pro and cons are fiercely disputed, whereas Europe as a common project seems to hardly matter. The inherent tensions between having an undoubtedly global position and – compared to that – a narrow-mindedness towards its direct European neighbours and a common Europe was the main reason for choosing the UK with its capital London as one of the venues of *Europe (to the power of) n*.

http://www.london.gov.uk

ROYAL COLLEGE OF ART

THE EUROPA TRIANGLE

The Europa Triangle was an exhibition in which all the works referred to triangles, pyramids, and similar forms. This could be considered as the most base level of curating; simply bringing together works on the basis of formal similarities. However, this apparent simplicity can often be the best way to address something highly complex, and so beneath the surface, *The Europa Triangle* is as much about the way we try to rationalise and shape the social and political world we live in. The triangles in this exhibition are not just geometric forms but conceptual models that relate to various aspects of how we organise society on different levels. It was surprisingly straightforward to make visible the possibility of such a typology and proves true that pyramids, in particular, can be found in various registers of social modelling.

The proposition of looking at various levels of subjectivity and governance is important in this exhibition. While it might have been more significant to the public to look at the work itself, the exhibition's structuring was as much under scrutiny asking: Who gets to speak when? Who really writes such scenarios? And what roles can I give over to others both selfishly and altruistically? What can I do for myself? This ran throughout the project – not just in the gallery, but also in the making of the show.

Kit Hammonds

SLAVS AND TATARS
Triangulation (Not Moscow, Not Mecca),
2011

27

Taking place in the Dyson Galleries at the Royal College of Art, the exhibition brought together works of art and design by Oliver Klimpel, Marisol Malatesta, Nils Norman, Diego Santomé, Slavs and Tatars, Christian Teckert, Lincoln Tobier, Daniel James Wilkinson, and Hannes Zebedin.

The display also included contributions from others, and the exhibition is only a part of the story. There was an aim to use the exhibition itself as a model for social orders. Many debates take place over the relationship between art and exhibitions, usually articulated more as a hierarchy between artist and curator. Instead of the exhibition being an end point that articulates a thesis of the curator, here it is taken to be the starting point for the curator to reflect on ideas through the works of art and the stories they tell. More importantly, it is an opportunity to use the exhibition as a point around which people are organised through various means – some planned, others accidental.

These contributions included the installation of the artworks by Marisol Malatesta, and curatorial decisions were devolved to Sunny Chueng, Ruth Lie, Christina Milliare, Lena Mohamed, Melanie Pocock, and Sacha Waldron, a group of students from the Inspire programme. Research material contributed by other Curating Contemporary Art students Hannah Conroy, Rachel Falconer, and Juste Kostikoviate – the latter presenting poetry by Karlis Verdinsh and Arturs Punte – was also displayed in the exhibition. Visitors and staff –

including Elena Kuri-Horri, Augustina Matusevičiūtė, and the security guards Shah, Jameel and Rao – were among the casual community that formed around the exhibition. They were asked to make aesthetic decisions such as the choice of colours for the publication and walls, or the location of signage. Therefore, the project has involved a number of people in the decision-making process in both contingent and planned ways. While ultimately one might still locate the strategy for this exhibition in the curator's remit, there have been decisive moments played out by others. On one side, there is the curator and the overarching project, the influence of the artistic director, the designer and the architect, and of those involved in the management of the project – within and adjunct to the Goethe-Institut and also the bureaucracy of the Royal College of Art. On another, there are the artists whose work predates, was made during, or has resulted from the exhibition.

The project comes to a close with a book that tells some of these stories, amplified through fictions drawn from the work of the artists, from the research, and from the reading around the show.

Artists:
Oliver Klimpel, Marisol Malatesta, Nils Norman, Diego Santomé, Slavs and Tatars, Christian Teckert, Lincoln Tobier, Daniel Wilkinson, Hannes Zebedin

HANNES ZEBEDIN
What's Happening Tottenham?, 20
(installation view)
Blind But Awake (Coincidental
Harmony Monument #1), 2012
(detail)

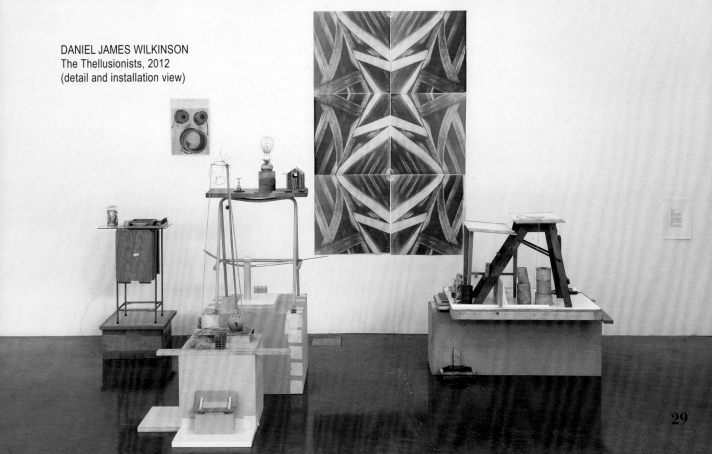

DANIEL JAMES WILKINSON
The Thellusionists, 2012
(detail and installation view)

HANNES ZEBEDIN
What's Happening Tottenham?, 2012
(installation view)

THE
EUROPA
TRIANGLE

18 July – 18 August
en Thursday – Saturday, 12–6pm
Admission free

MARISOL MALATESTA
Tildados de mondernos, 2011
Calvary from Right to Left, 2011
M.–.R.–.H.–., 2012

Display Elements designed by Christian Teckert, displaying research into triangulation, pyramid structures and sand heaps by Kit Hammonds and Rachel Falconer, Hannah Conroy and Juste Kostikoviate

Installation shot showing Europe^n tables based on the visual identity designed by Oliver Klimpel

On the table is poetry by Karlis Verdinsh and Arturs Punte (foreground) and "The Paragon Press" by Daniel James Wilkinson (background)

Sabine Hentzsch, Goethe-Institut London

After the opening festival in Berlin, the first stop for the trans-regional art project *Europe (to the power of) n* was in London. Disregarding the various controversies about the EU and the euro in the political arena, Europe is not the dominant issue in the British capital. It is precisely for this reason that we wanted to send a signal through the means of art to initiate a process of reflection on the central issues of the exhibition. As a country, the United Kingdom does not perceive Europe as a community it belongs to, quite the contrary: it sets itself apart from Europe to highlight its distinctive status. No one would ever regard the United Kingdom as on the periphery in either a geographical or a cultural sense, and yet at times it feels outside of Europe. The Royal College of Art took the exhibition, *The Europa Triangle,* as an opportunity to inaugurate its new building in London's Battersea. The so-called Dyson Building with its glass front is eye-catching and very effective at attracting passersby. However, in July and August 2012 the entire city was focused on the great sporting event of the year – the Olympic Games – which meant that public response was well below our expectations. *The Europa Triangle* can nevertheless be considered as the beginning of a new reflection on a wide range of issues on Europe through art, which simultaneously links the past with the present.

Cover motif of accompanying publication by Kit Hammonds

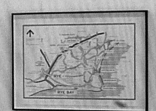

NILS NORMAN
Romney Reborn, 1996–2012
The Commune of Lydd, 2012
The Jury's Gap Phalanstery, 2012

MARISOL MALATESTA
Tolerencia no. 18, 2012
Under the Influence, 2012
Three Way Progression, 2012
From the Last Landowner, 2012
Design, Calculation and
Optimisation, 2012

34

SPECULATION AND IMPLEMENTATION

Barbara Steiner

Altogether there are fifteen curators,127 artists, three architects and twelve designers, two programmers, eleven venues, two magazines, eleven institutions involved in the implementation of *Europe (to the power of) n* – not to forget the regional and the local Goethe-Institutes and the supporters: the Cultural Programme of the European Union, the Robert Bosch Foundation, and the Allianz Cultural Foundation. The sheer numbers show a multiplicity of views that is essential for this project. Divided into two parts – a prologue, *Scenarios about Europe*, and an exhibition series, *Europe (to the power of) n* – the project has asked how to approach the topic of Europe from the perspective of the visual arts.

The prologue took place at the Museum of Contemporary Art in Leipzig, Germany, between September 2011 and March 2012. Speculative in nature, it resulted in a series of spatial presentations and a book, which comprises thirty reflections about Europe by fifty-one artists and writers revolving around the relationship between the individual and society, forms of social organisation and of living together. In addition, possibilities for a common visual and spatial identity, which take heterogeneity as a point of departure, were tested and reflected upon.

In both, continuation and dissociation, *Europe (to the power of) n* must be seen as manifestation of thoughts investigated in Leipzig and their translation into very specific political, economic, social, or cultural contexts. Under the title *The Europa Triangle*, in which all the works referred to triangles, pyramids and similar forms, the London curator brought together various models in society, politics and economics that show how the social and political world we live in is shaped and rationalised. In Minsk the relationship of Belarus to Europe and the construction of a Belarusian identity stood at the forefront of interest: The exhibition entitled *West of East* introduced a reversed view of Europe as being a small western appendix on the Eurasian continent stretching from the Urals to the Atlantic, with Belarus in the middle. The exhibition in Łódź, *Untimely Stories*, took a closer look into post-colonial discourses assuming that ideas and solutions on which the political project Europe is based and carried out in the form of the European Union, are losing their validity. Instead, the artists involved addressed transformations of the current geopolitical relations between the centres and the peripheries. The İstanbul project addressed under the title *Measure* fortification processes in Europe, which have become a contentious issue in Turkey since its accession negotiations. Carried out in public space, in the streets on outdoor advertising boards, and in the subway the project's main topic was dedicated to those who lost their lives on their way to the European Union. Black and white posters listed the people, their names, ages, and places of origin – if known – and the circumstances of their death. Under the title *Learning for Life* the Norwegian curator focused on primary school, on the relationship between freedom and discipline, asking what kind of citizens have been created within the current school system, and questioning tendencies that are concerned solely with measurable results and not with nurturing free individuals. The Novi Sad exhibition *Asymmetric Europe* asked what is now part of the European identity on the borderlines of South-East Europe, examining the relationship between symmetric and asymmetric identities in contemporary Europe. In Brussels the project took place in the European district and aimed at reflecting on *Cultural Freedom in Europe* from various perspectives. The choice of the Committee of the Regions and the European Social and Economic Committee as exhibition sites was testing the possibilities of contemporary art within a highly regulated environment. In Donostia – San Sebastián various concepts of Europe were discussed taking into consideration the role of culture in general and that of contemporary art in particular. *Constellation Europe* aimed at thinking Europe as an imaginary network of arbitrary identities, which, nevertheless, constitute an order.

The Chinese contribution entitled *Does Europe matter?* closed the series of exhibitions within the framework of *Europe (to the power of) n* with an exhibition, a conference at Vitamin Creative Space in Beijing, an online reader produced by the Contemporary Art Center in Taipei, and an excerpt of the reader in the Taiwanese Artco Monthly Magazine. All curators of *Europe (to the power of) n* were invited to choose one artwork from their own exhibition to be presented in Beijing. However, there was one important difference: The artworks had to be reproductions. This offered the chance not only to look at the project from a distant point of view, but also to re-examine and reflect upon the series of exhibitions that took place at various locations. In addition, the status of the original – still very important in Europe – was challenged through displaying only reproductions.

Following pages:
FLORIAN GÖTHNER
Neighbours, 2012
(film stills)

The film *Neighbours* (4 min) by Florian Göthner was developed for the project *Europe (to the power of) n* and screened for the first time at Haus der Kulturen der Welt in June 2012. It invokes closeness and distance at once. The collages of landscapes, which seem to be real, are "ghost images", virtual spaces with open interfaces and connections.

For the book a range of stills from the film were chosen to make associations with the places, playing with signifiers, likelihood and memory. Owed more to imagination than facts Beijing, Brussels, Høvikodden / Oslo, İstanbul, Łódź, London, Minsk, Novi Sad, and Donostia – San Sebastián emerge and disappear, remaining ambiguous and contingent. Göthner's film stills do not only mark the unfeasibility of adequate representation – they offer multiple spaces that interconnect.

Minsk / Vilnius*

The question of whether the Ukraine (with Kiev) or Belarus (with Minsk) should be one venue of *Europe (to the power of) n* remained undecided for a while. Although different in many regards, both share the tension between pro-European and pro-Russian voices and an orientation to different political and cultural spheres. And both are currently under authoritarian rules. Finally, the decision for Belarus was made on the basis of its almost hermetically sealed off position in the midst of Europe. The territory of present-day Belarus underwent various rules: from being part of the Grand Duchy of Lithuania and the Polish-Lithuanian Commonwealth to being part of the Russian Empire, the Duchy of Warsaw and later of the Soviet Union. Almost fully destroyed by the German Armed Forces, Minsk was rebuilt after World War II and the historic centre was replaced by Soviet-style architecture and urban planning. Until 1991, Minsk was the capital of the Belarusian Soviet Socialist Republic. Following Belarusia's independence, Minsk became the centre of the new state and Alexander Grigoryevich Lukashenko has been its President since 1994. Lukashenko introduced economic integration with the Russian Federation and built strong ties with countries of the Commonwealth of independent states – former Soviet republics such as Armenia, Azerbaijan, Kazakhstan, Moldova, Turkmenistan, Uzbekistan.

*Actually, the project *Europe (to the power of) n* was not only carried out in Minsk but also in Vilnius, where the exiled Belarusian European Humanities University is located. The European Humanities University (EHU) is a private, non-profit arts university founded in Minsk in 1992. Celebrating its 20th anniversary in 2012, EHU has been headquartered in Vilnius, Lithuania, since authorities expelled it from Belarus in 2004. The EHU was one of the collaboration partners within the frame *Europe (to the power of) n*.

http://minsk.gov.by/en/   http://www.ehu.lt/en/

WEST OF EAST

GALLERY Ў MINSK

AND

NATIONAL GALLERY OF ART
VILNIUS, CINEMA SPACE

SERGEY SHABOHIN
We Are Stern Consumers Of Cultural
Revolutions, 2012
(installation view and detail)

Lena Prents

The exhibition *West of East* at Gallery Ў in Minsk, along with the programme accompanying it, was dedicated to the changeable and widely discussed relationship between Belarus and Europe. In Belarusian terminology, the word "West" still stands for a better and more just way of life. More recently, an inflationary use of the attribute "European" can also be observed. Belarus is situated more or less at the centre of the Eurasian landmass, between the Urals and the Atlantic. Its geographical location is seen as an argument for its affiliation with "Europe", in contrast to its insignificant position of marginalisation and exclusion, whether this is perceived or real.

Historically, there are many associations with Europe: the demand for freedom, democracy, human rights, the spirit of enlightenment, and a system that obeys the principles of rationality. Belarusian intellectuals relate these ideas of Europe to the current political and social system in Belarus. However, during the Age of Enlightenment, when European ideals were being formulated, an ideological division of the continent manifested itself. Western Europe was conceived as standing at the height of civilisation, whereas Eastern Europe was considered backward. This evaluation, with which the West clearly disparaged the East, was often also adopted in the East in the form of a recurrent condemnation of Eastern conditions and a glorification of life in the West.

The title of the exhibition, *West of East,* made a conscious reference to this comparative view. Local perspectives were supplemented by a view inspired by the West. The works of art shown in the exhibition examined aspects that are automatically claimed or considered to be "European". But who or what really belongs to Europe? Who decides? Is contemporary Europe an ideal? What merit can be given to "European values"? Is Europe primarily a union of economic interests? What significance does culture have in the European Community? The six sections of the exhibition – economy, identity, culture, language, education, and community – were concerned with European realities that cannot always be brought into line with the unreserved pathos that often arises when proclamations of European community and solidarity are made.

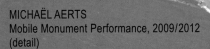

MICHAËL AERTS
Mobile Monument Performance, 2009/2012
(detail)

GOLDIN+SENNEBY
Not Approved: Field Inspection
Photographs Of Rejected
Landscape Features, 2009
(installation view and detail)

48

ANDREI LIANKEVICH
Double Heroes, 2012

MICHAËL AERTS
Mobile Monument Performance,
2009/2012
(installation view)

6

СУПОЛЬНАСЦЬ

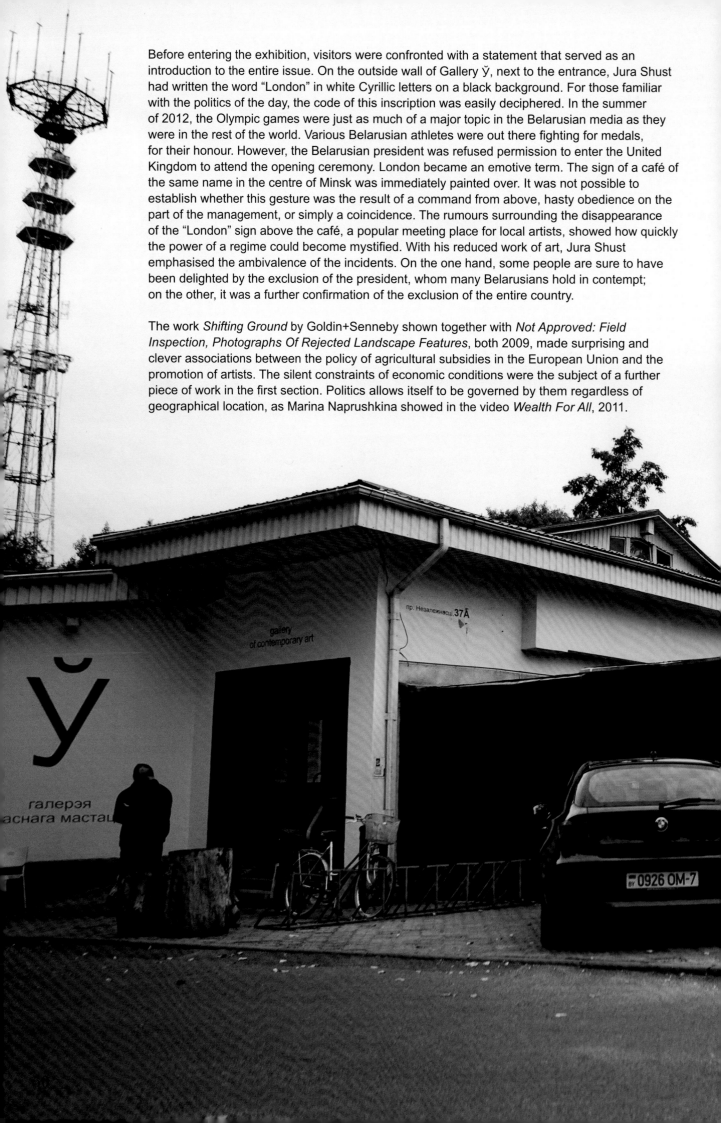

Before entering the exhibition, visitors were confronted with a statement that served as an introduction to the entire issue. On the outside wall of Gallery ў, next to the entrance, Jura Shust had written the word "London" in white Cyrillic letters on a black background. For those familiar with the politics of the day, the code of this inscription was easily deciphered. In the summer of 2012, the Olympic games were just as much of a major topic in the Belarusian media as they were in the rest of the world. Various Belarusian athletes were out there fighting for medals, for their honour. However, the Belarusian president was refused permission to enter the United Kingdom to attend the opening ceremony. London became an emotive term. The sign of a café of the same name in the centre of Minsk was immediately painted over. It was not possible to establish whether this gesture was the result of a command from above, hasty obedience on the part of the management, or simply a coincidence. The rumours surrounding the disappearance of the "London" sign above the café, a popular meeting place for local artists, showed how quickly the power of a regime could become mystified. With his reduced work of art, Jura Shust emphasised the ambivalence of the incidents. On the one hand, some people are sure to have been delighted by the exclusion of the president, whom many Belarusians hold in contempt; on the other, it was a further confirmation of the exclusion of the entire country.

The work *Shifting Ground* by Goldin+Senneby shown together with *Not Approved: Field Inspection, Photographs Of Rejected Landscape Features*, both 2009, made surprising and clever associations between the policy of agricultural subsidies in the European Union and the promotion of artists. The silent constraints of economic conditions were the subject of a further piece of work in the first section. Politics allows itself to be governed by them regardless of geographical location, as Marina Naprushkina showed in the video *Wealth For All*, 2011.

Perhaps the vaguest term used in relation to Europe – although it is very common and used at almost any opportunity – is that of "European identity". "Identity" and "Europe" are both terms that are difficult to grasp, let alone in combination with one another. And identity is something that is not so easy to assess. If someone refers to it, or even wishes to create it, he or she is certainly more likely to be concerned with a diffuse, but clearly affirmative feeling than with a rational declaration based on a common project. In his work *Double Heroes*, 2012, the Belarusian photographer Andrei Liankevich showed how the very modern Belarusian identity is built on the Soviet identity, and how the heroic victory in the Great Patriotic War is exploited without question in order to create it. On the other hand, the Japanese artist Asako Iwama showed in her cooking performance in Minsk entitled *She knows only what he knows that she knows he knows only what she knows that he knows* the constructability of identity by consciously breaking through basic orientations.

The sections "Culture" and "Language" picked out two further controversial Belarusian phenomena as central themes. In the installation *We Are Stern Consumers Of Cultural Revolutions*, 2012, Sergey Shabohin commented on the ambivalent heritage of the avant-garde, which made a brief appearance at the art school in Vitebsk in Belarus in the 1920s. Today, the avant-garde is re-emerging as part of mass culture and as a design for the masses. In his films *Language*

JURA SHUST
London, 2012
(wall painting)

MARINA NAPRUSHKINA
Wealth For All, 2011
(installation view)

Lessons, 2011, and *Palipaduazennije*, 2012, Aleksander Komarov turned his attention to language as an idea that must not necessarily separate people, but which could develop a potential for breaking new ground.

Ane Hjort Guttu's film *Freedom Requires Free People*, 2011, made a strong plea for a free education system based on self-determination. Finally, in the section "Community", Michaël Aerts invited various groups to take part in a *Mobile Monument Performance*.

Artists:
Michaël Aerts, Goldin+Senneby, Ane Hjort Guttu,
Asako Iwama, Aleksander Komarov, Andrei Liankevich,
Marina Naprushkina, Sergey Shabohin, Jura Shust

Frank Baumann, Goethe-Institut Minsk

Minsk, the capital of Belarus, was the third stop of the art project *Europe (to the power of) n*. At the time of the exhibition at the non-state-owned Gallery Ў in September 2012, it seemed that things were returning to a state of equilibrium after a period of chaos: the ambassadors of the EU member states, who collectively left in February in protest of the country, had returned and the disastrous consequences of the devaluation of the national currency by nearly 300 per cent along with the price increases of 2011 had yielded a growth rate of 10 per cent, which was about the same as it was before the crisis. Many artists and intellectuals asked themselves where things would go from here. It was "business as usual" for some, but for others it was the right time to take stock. "Europe" is neither an enemy nor a saviour for most Belarusians, but it embodies the hope for a better future based on their common European past. While the official policy of the country promotes integration into the "Eurasian" economic and cultural space, and thus into the open arms of Russia, many people would say if asked, that the political, economic, and cultural future of the country lies rather in closer co-operation with Central and Western Europe. Against this broad, almost existential background, the Minsk exhibition lead only a small portion of the public into a discussion on what "Europe" is or could be. A curatorial-intellectual approach that organically conveys discourse rather than offering answers does not need a majority to legitimise itself. The question is rather whether the exhibition could justify its claim as an artistic snapshot of selective social analyses of European polyphony through preserving a certain substantive rigour. In part, one got the impression that it had.

The place was well chosen and the interest shown by the public at the opening was substantial. A calculated scandal involving the large-scale installation by the photographer Andrei Liankevich, showing the same man standing next to himself in the uniforms of the German Wehrmacht (German Armed Forces) and the Red Army, was kept just within reasonable limits. This had probably not so much to do with the visitors ignoring the interesting artistic approach in favour of the potential for provocation, but rather because Belarusians associate "Europe", the exhibition's lowest common denominator, with something else. "Europe" is something that remains and must remain wherever possible vague. This is why the subject could not be fully met in *Europe (to the power of) n*. But that alone is indeed a result, which means that the effort put in by all participants was worth it.

Johanna M. Keller, Goethe-Institut Vilnius

It is somewhat symbolic for Lithuania's self-perception as advocate of Belarus within the EU that the Belarusian part of *Europe (to the power of) n* took place both in Minsk and Vilnius. Surprisingly enough for an outsider imagining "Europe's last dictatorship" being indeterminably far, the geographical distance between the capitals is only 180 kilometres – and thus the project's events became a metaphor for all those Belarusians constantly commuting between the two cities as well as for those working and living outside their home country. It was mostly a mix of young Belarusians and Lithuanians that came together at the National Gallery of Art in Vilnius in November 2012 to have a closer look at the urban transformation of Berlin.

The events were organised by the Contemporary Art Study Centre at the European Humanities University, a Belarusian university in exile in Vilnius. Florian Wüst presented the film *After Effect* by Stephan Geene. Stefan Rusu's film *Reclaiming the City* and the resulting question of the transformation of public space is relevant both for Minsk and for Vilnius. In Vilnius, art in public space is more and more commercialised, which invites for a critical perspective on the economic implications of the creative and cultural industries. In Minsk, the question remains how public space can be used at all vis-à-vis the regime's interpretational power.

After Effect

A film by Stephan Geene. D 2007, 75 min. With an introduction and talk by Florian Wüst, artist and film curator, Berlin

28. November   17:00   National Art Gallery   Konstitucijos g. 22

Reclaiming the City

A film by Stefan Rusu. MD/RO 2012, 64 min. With a following talk with Stefan Rusu, artist and curator, Chisinau/Bucharest

29. November   17:00   National Art Gallery   Konstitucijos g. 22

The film programme *Urban Transformations in Europe: The Myth and the Reality of Berlin as "poor yet sexy"* was a complementary event to *West of East. An Exhibition on Europe in six Chapters* in Minsk. It took place at the National Gallery of Art Vilnius on 28 and 29 November 2012, and was connected with the Colloquium Vilnensis of the Center for German Studies at the European Humanities University in Vilnius. The film programme critically examined the role of the creative and cultural industries in city development.

Łódź

Compared to the first half of the 20th century, the importance of today's Łódź is small. In the 19th and early 20th centuries, its textile industry had attracted a lot of immigrants from all over Europe. By the beginning of World War I, it had become one of the most densely populated industrial cities in the world with a very heterogeneous population with a large Jewish community. In the Holocaust, the Jewish population of Łódź was almost wiped out. After 1990, the textile industry declined dramatically and the city has undergone an enormous transformation. One significant expression of this is the conversion of the largest 19th-century textile factory complex, which was built by Izrael Poznanski, into the shopping mall "Manufaktura". Apart from shopping facilities, it hosts one branch of the Muzeum Sztuki – a museum famous for its outstanding collection of avant-garde art and its commitment to contemporary art. In short, not only did Łódź´s triple transformation from capitalism to socialism (communism) and back to capitalism make its participation in *Europe (to the power of) n* relevant, but also its transition from a cosmopolitan city at the centre of attention, to its current position on the periphery.

http://uml.lodz.pl/

MUZEUM SZTUKI

UNTIMELY STORIES

ANIKÓ LORÁNT AND TAMÁS KASZÁS
(EX-ARTISTS COLLECTIVE)
Famine Food, since 2011
(installation view)

GAST BOUSCHET & NADINE HILBERT
A Planet (Svínafellsjökull, Iceland)
June 2011– June 2012

The exhibition *Untimely Stories* and the accompanying catalogue were an attempt to recognise
the current and forthcoming situation of Europe
through art. At a time when the social contracts
and ideas that the European model had been
based on are eroding and, thus, requiring new
ideas for the future, art might offer diagnoses and
suppositions without making claims to being
a solution to current problems. Therefore, our aim
was to think of the politics of art that (contrary
to conventional politics) makes a conscious use
of fiction in which it sees the function of truth.
It creates, stages, and performs stories, which may
signal the truth of what is contemporary or
upcoming. For the possible interpretation of the
relations within the web of the various artistic
narratives featured in the exhibition we proposed
the concept of *untimeliness*.

ANIKÓ LORÁNT AND TAMÁS KASZÁS
(EX-ARTISTS COLLECTIVE)
Famine Food, since 2011
(installation view and detail)

According to Friedrich Nietzsche, to act "untimely" is to act counter to our time and thereby act on our time, and thus "for the benefit of a time to come". Expanding upon Nietzsche's theory, Giorgio Agamben identifies the untimely with the contemporary. According to him, a person who is truly contemporary goes beyond his or her time, beyond the present moment, beyond the pragmatic logics of punctuality. Those who perfectly inscribe themselves into the present are unable to see the present. Only an active and often conflicting attitude with one's time makes it possible to recognise it properly and act accordingly, in agreement with a subjectively perceived truth about this time. The works presented in the exhibition are untimely in this sense. They become contemporary by means of going beyond their own moment in time. They are an act of opening to that which is to come, and to the upcoming effects of our past.

Through the artistic narratives in the exhibition, there was an attempt to challenge thinking on some widely discussed currents in Europe today, but also to provoke reflections on what is yet unknown, ambivalent, or obscured. *Untimely Stories* reversed Europe's present dominant, integration-driven economism, in which the management of resources is construed in a highly limited way, opposing it with a general economy (which also includes gift and hospitality economies, the politics of friendship, the critique of non-human reason, ecology, non-systemic modes of survival). The exhibition also proposed a reversal of geopolitical relationships, determining dependencies between centres and peripheries. Therefore, it tried to confront Europe's Western-centric and colonial legacy and emphasised knowledge, skills, and traditions reaching beyond the established trajectories of the outdated imperial influence, which still seem to shape hierarchies of cultural values, while losing its economic foundations. The artists' works addressed in particular an urgency of adaptation to that which is unforeseeable, uncanny and yet unrecognised in the traditions of Western European modernity, as well as in the current models of governance and society.

However, the exhibition did not provide solutions to be pragmatically applied or visions to be realised in the future. Rather, it suggested ways in which we could think, see and feel in order to make a different kind of action possible. The fictions created by the artists were not unified into a single overarching narrative or subsumed into a totality. Rather, they were brought together and juxtaposed in order to create a polyphony of voices. This polyphony did not become a cacophony, because the voices were mediated, or orchestrated, as it were, by Krzysztof Skoczylas's exhibition architecture. His unique design enhanced and unleashed every artwork's inherent potential to establish relationships and facilitate encounters. Thanks to the architecture, the exhibition became a space where different voices could meet, without reducing their diversity, or, rather, without muting the power of the truth of singularity expressed by each of them. This was made possible by a specific mood that established a common dimension between the works. Thus, communication took place in a non-discursive medium, pre-linguistic and pre-conscious, one could say, and one based on affects and impressions (the pure language sought by Benjamin?). The exhibition architecture made it possible to highlight and communicate this pre-linguistic and pre-conscious medium of the mood, which each of the presented works uses in its own way.

By highlighting and amplifying this aspect, the exhibition achieved what proved its weakest and, at the same time, its strongest point. This truly symbolic act (in the double meaning of the term as defined by Kenneth Burke) was the suspension of action. What became untimely in the exhibition was a sense of anticipation, not so much of the performance of a task or fulfilment of a desire, but rather of the coming of the inevitable, unknown and unpredictable. The suspension of action in which this anticipation arose revoked the feeling of anxiety and hope usually associated with it, replacing it with an affirmation of that which is yet to come. The anticipation was thus combined with a readiness to meet an infinite number of future scenarios for Europe and the world.

Artists and groups:
Akademia Ruchu, Mohamed Bourouissa, Gast Bouschet & Nadine Hilbert, Jérémie Boyard, Peter Friedl, Jens Haaning, Agnieszka Kalinowska, Aleksander Komarov, KwieKulik, Anikó Lóránt & Tamás Kaszás (ex-artists collective), Nástio Mosquito, Ahmet Öğüt, Wendelien van Oldenborgh, Janek Simon, Slavs and Tatars, Mona Vătămanu & Florin Tudor

Exhibition architecture:
Krzysztof Skoczylas

Catalogue design by
Jakub de Barbaro

Niewczesne
Historie

Untimely
Stories

Nie wiedzielibyśmy, jaki sens ziałaby sztuka w naszych czasach, jak nie ten, by działać w nich niewcześnie – to znaczy wbrew czasowi i przez to na czas i, mamy nadzieję, na korzyść czasu, który przyjdzie.

We would not know what point would the art have in our times if not the one to act within them in untimely manner – that is against the time and by that on time and, we hope, on the benefit of the time that is to come.

ALEKSANDER KOMAROV
Palipaduazennije, 2011
(background)

WENDELIEN VAN OLDENBORGH
Supposing I Love You. And You Also
Love Me. 2011
(installation view)

NÁSTIO MOSQUITO
Continent, 2010

PETER FRIEDL
Theory of Justice, 2008
(foreground)

AHMET ÖĞÜT
Mutual Issues, Inventive Acts, 2008

Europe (to the power of) n: At the Heart of Contemporaneity
Untimely Stories at Muzeum Sztuki in Łódź

Georg Blochmann, Goethe-Institut Warsaw

The Polish language has its very own word for "Deutschland" – not "Germania", not "Alemania", but "Niemcy". "Niemiec", a German, is someone who cannot speak, who is mute, because he simply fails to master Polish phonetics. "Łódź" in Polish sounds soft and melodious; most Germans end up pronouncing it in a fairly unappealing way: "Lotsch". For five years, from 1939 until 1944, they even called it "Litzmannstadt", depressingly notorious as one of the centres of Nazi terror on Polish soil. Łódź proudly describes itself as the "city of four cultures". Poles, Germans, Jews, and Russians lived here in comparative harmony, as they did in so many parts of this country. Łódź was rich in the 19th century, when it was the hub of the Polish textile industry, as factory buildings, villas, and town houses in the city centre still testify today – as does the wonderful collection of masterpieces from the first half of the 20th century, which artists brought together here and which were successfully hidden from the Nazis; art that sought to critically examine society, art that was progressive, utopian – European. Łódź is situated almost precisely in Poland's geographical centre, and the Muzeum Sztuki is regarded as being one of the most outstanding centres of contemporary art in the country, indeed in all of Europe. The museum's curators strive for contemporaneity in the sense of visionary participation in a discourse engaged in by society as a whole.

More than twenty years after the political transformation of 1989, Poland has returned to Europe. The many young artists and intellectuals who have travelled from nearby Warsaw to attend the opening of *Untimely Stories* in Łódź do not need to be persuaded of the European idea. This idea, however, is about more than merely the free movement of people, goods, and services. The exhibition's title is a quotation from Giorgio Agamben: contemporaneity does not mean remaining stubbornly in the present, but reaching out for the potential of that which is to come. The artists represented in the exhibition are reclaiming this visionary interpretive predominance – in diverse ways and from diverse perspectives. Geopolitical definitions of periphery and centre become meaningless. The exhibition's visual worlds develop an enormous captivating power and we, the visitors, ponder on Europe.

JÉRÉMIE BOYARD
On the Verge of a Down, 2010

previous and following pages:
FLORIAN GÖTHNER
Neighbours, 2012
(film stills)

70

EUROPE, THE EUROPEAN UNION, AND ART

TONE HANSEN: Europe or, more specifically, the European Union as we face it from Oslo is a regulative body that takes bureaucratic control of one institution after another. Related to that, the question of education has become a European subject, and even here we are to obey bureaucratic ideas of control and measurable results. We are in many ways losing the ability of looking at the larger goals as we are forced to deal with the smaller ones, like how good each child is at mathematics, and not with ideology or politics of education. This is why I think that looking at the ideology of teaching and education is important and an effective form of social critique. And this is what we did with our project. First of all, we focused on primary education, because that is where the future workforce is being formed and schools are incredibly powerful ideological tools. Secondly, have already focused a lot on the consequences of the Bologna Process and its effect on art education. We wanted to investigate a subject that relates to all people in Europe: how our young generation is being formed and who decides about this formation.

FILIP LUYCKX: Most people might agree on the importance of a European community, but feel little interest for the daily politics and the bureaucratic rules of the European Union. The EU has a very limited concept of Europe, which has been in constant evolution since its foundation in 1958. But when we start to understand Europe as a continent bearing the individual interests of more than a billion human beings, the concept is so overwhelming that nobody can conceive what we are really speaking about when we speak of Europe. The regions are very different. There are so many issues and opinions existing close to each other. That is why we can only imagine Europe on an abstract level. Most aspects of Europe lie beyond European politics, but will inevitably contribute to shaping the future of the continent.

PEIO AGUIRRE: "Europe" is both concrete when it comes to the European Union and abstract when it comes to Europe as a concept. Since our first meeting in Munich in summer 2010, the topic of Europe has become more and more present on the world's political agenda. I remember that the Greek crisis was already burning at that time. Italy was hit by the financial crisis later and more recently Spain. Offensive and reactionary terms such as PIGS have been coined since then. The timeline of *Europe (to the power of) n* has coincided with this debate and with the crisis of Europe and the European Union. This has been very challenging for our project. However, the most difficult task for me was to connect its structure, which mimics at the level of form some complexities of Europe, with the knowledge and experience of the viewer to raise a debate about Europe and not just about financial problems in the EU.

JUN YANG: For me, it is important not to narrow Europe down to the European Union. I am interested in Europe's "individualism" and its attempts of forming a group, which is mirrored somehow in our common project, too. Maybe it is the view from a person having the most distant point and perspective to look at Europe: if Europe is a combination of individuals, of individual single identities, and if *Europe (to the power of) n* is a project on how to think of these single identities and a unified identity, then this suggests itself to be reflected in the structure and the working method of the project – with several curators, several locations, and different separate projects. One could also say that if Europe is a model of how individual identities can co-exist and work together on different levels, then perhaps *Europe (to the power of) n* was also a model or testing ground for how different individuals within contemporary art and cultural production can work together and create a multi-level exhibition series.

KIT HAMMONDS: The proposition of looking at various levels of subjectivity and governance is important. This was reflected on in my exhibition: what roles can I give over to others both selfishly and altruistically? What can I do for myself? This ran throughout the making of my show in London. And this was also an important issue of *Europe (to the power of) n:* How much does one give up or, I suppose, give up oneself? People have personality traits – everybody has an ego. So it is interesting to reflect on that. Of course, I am also absolutely aware that a group can be very egotistical. It paints a sort of particular picture even though it disguises the fact that it is quite controlled as well. Actually, the biggest challenge of being part of the group was when you keep hitting the point where you realise you are being a little conservative yourself. And Miško is particularly good at reminding me of this (laughter). Every time I felt I was breaking my own boundaries, he was already four steps ahead of me. It is definitely interesting to mirror yourself against your colleagues in that way, in the project, in your own approach, in communication.

MIŠKO ŠUVAKOVIĆ: For me, it was really important that the project was not just about a presentation of artworks, famous curators, or a celebration of art, but instead it was the starting point for a dialogue – a political, cultural, and artistic dialogue. Art is, for me in this moment, a social vehicle, particularly a mode of rediscovering the human condition. This is not about who is right – Germans, Serbians, or Croatians, or … – but about how to produce a dialogue and the conditions of real social situations, which make the dialogue possible. And, for me, the project *Europe (to the power of) n* offers the possibility for having a dialogue on different levels, be it the personal dialogue between people, curators, and artists, or the dialogue between artworks – it is more than the presentation of artworks or the production of a good exhibition. Actually, it fulfills my desire for emancipatory politics through art.

FILIP LUYCKX: Without doubt, art can have an important role in society, although I see a problem in the fact that politicians are so far away from art and artists. They do not have an interest in having a dialogue with them. Look at the heart of Europe in Brussels. There you find tightly closed off administrative buildings and a lack of visual culture in general. You feel the one-dimensional education that the European managers received at the universities: there are plenty of facilities for conferences, meetings, and receptions, but no space for artistic experience accessible to the public. Maybe from the 20th century they inherited a fear to demonstrate the external signs of representation? Large amounts of money are spent on office buildings, bureaucratic procedures, and internal events. Why not offer an image of cultural creativity to the outside world?

MIŠKO ŠUVAKOVIĆ: Unfortunately, today everybody speaks about economic, political, and national problems, but not about human conditions and about possibilities for becoming emancipated from them. This is why Hannah Arendt is so important for me and why a portrait of her became a part of the triptych produced by *Provisional SALTA Ensemble* for the Novi Sad exhibition. I think, her notion of politics is very important for our time and for contemporary art. It is not Michel Foucault's notion of structural power, it is not the Marxist notions of class, personal, or economic power, it is the idea of will for new social relations, because she said "politics is the event of the human condition, of human relations". And, for me, Arendt is symbolically and conceptually important for this project evolving with a narrative of Europe rooted in a struggle for real human life.

ESRA SARIGEDIK ÖKTEM: I am interested in what a narrative of Europe could be. In my projects, I tried to look at Europe from different angles. First, I was really trying to understand what Europe is for myself. So I started with a kind of domestic need and set the scene for a domestic Turkish scenario referencing the history of coffee. The first scenario included Lars von Trier's movie *Europa* and Joanna Rajkowska's photograph from the Old Library in Konja having Walter Benjamin's "Task of the Translator" in mind. Then, together with the artist and cook Asako Iwama, I was looking into immigration, and with me as a Turkish woman and Iwama as a Japanese woman, we had a closer look into our different perceptions and certainly also prejudgments of how Europe is looking at us or how we are looking at Europe. It was a double-sided approach – neither side innocent. The third approach addressed the attributes and categorisations of how Filipino women in Israel are looked at and how they look at their Israeli hosts, how Turkish female artists are looked at and how they look at European collectors. CANAN was really playing with this.

LENA PRENTS: What you are saying here raises not only the question of what Europe is or might be. It is related to identity issues as well. How do we define ourselves in relation to Europe? Where do we locate ourselves in Europe – at the fringes or outside? And how are we defined and located by others?

ESRA SARIGEDIK ÖKTEM: Talking about Europe in Turkey is difficult. Am I European or Ottoman – this was also a very interesting point for me, because I never feel European. Nevertheless, Turkey's potential entry into the European Union is a topic and with this, regulations and controls for tightened border control transform Europe into a fortress. After I had read *The Seventh Man,* a book in the form of photography and text on migrant workers in Europe first published in 1975, I started looking into the situation of current illegal immigration to Europe. It is quite interesting that migration has become such a problem in Turkey. The topic has really exploded and now it seems to be everywhere.

LENA PRENTS: I would like to pick up the aspect of being at the margin. Even though Belarus is approximately located in the midst of the European landmass between the Urals and the Atlantic, and even though this is quite often taken as an argument for being part of Europe, there is a constant debate about a felt or real marginal position and a search for a Belarusian identity. However, its conception varies a lot, because Belarus may be located in Europe, but does not participate with equal measure. My exhibition *West of East* responded to these issues. Actually the relationship of Europe to Belarus and the other way round was put on display seen against the light of Western and Eastern traditions and attributions.

JUN YANG: There is one aspect that sounds familiar to me: the trauma of not having an identity of one's own. Let us take the examples of Hong Kong as a former British colony, which is now under Chinese rule, and Taiwan with its former Dutch and Japanese occupation periods. In Taiwan's case one could even say the government now is the remains of the Nationalist Chinese Army occupation after the Second World War. They are seeking their identity under the big shadow of China, and China itself is rising from its trauma of being occupied and humiliated by Western, European forces in the last century, now regaining its strength and its self-confidence. These are "troubled" identities. Perhaps the most dominating and most interesting discussions at this moment within China, Hong Kong, and Taiwan are circling around cultural and national sovereignty and identity. I think the debates are still grounded in a Euro-centric postcolonial point of view and references to as well as emancipation from these discussions are needed in my opinion.

TONE HANSEN: In Europe, power relations regarding cultural hegemony have changed, too. In the beginning of the 20th century, Norway was a poor country testing its education system in continental Europe, and central Europe was the model both for forming a national identity and an educated nation. Still, education is a way out of poverty, but as has already been said, power relations have changed. This is also expressed in our project at the Henie-Onstad Kunstsenter: in the choice of artists from Turkey, the Netherlands, Sweden, Iran, Norway, Portugal, the USA, and Peru one can see that the question of freedom and discipline is an international subject, but that it also takes on a different form depending on country, region, climate, and culture. In the beginning, we focused mainly on the Scandinavian egalitarian school, the public school, but quickly we saw that many artists from many countries work on these issues and that ideology of education is something that many artists have focused on from many different angles.

JAROSŁAW LUBIAK: I agree, it is time to broaden our horizon: Joanna and I think that social contracts and ideas, which the European model had been based on, are eroding. Our exhibition *Untimely Stories* in

Łódź proposed, among a reversal of economic models, for instance towards gift and hospitality economies, a reversal of geopolitical relationships. Therefore, it tried to confront Europe's Western-centric and colonial legacy and emphasised knowledge, skills, and traditions. It reaches beyond the established trajectories of the outdated imperial influence, which still seem to shape hierarchies of cultural values while losing their economic foundations.

JUN YANG: I wish we would look at this from both sides: what can we learn from "Europe" and what can "Europe" learn from others. I am particularly interested in more permeable and less hermetic relationships, which allow creating debates and exchange about these issues and questions. As I said earlier, for me Europe is a model of how individual identities can co-exist and work together on different levels. This is nothing we should take for granted.

JOANNA SOKOŁOWSKA: I wish the postcolonial issues were addressed more. They appear here and there, but they were not really articulated in the seminars we did during *Europe (to the power of) n*. In Poland, this is an emerging topic right now. We are talking about Europe too much.

PEIO AGUIRRE: However, talking about Europe remains vague and talking about the European Union is too concrete and very often associated with regulation and bureaucratic control, as Tone said rightly in the beginning. I think we were all facing the problem of how to do an exhibition about such a heavy loaded subject like "Europa". My point of departure was that the subject itself cannot be represented, but the only thing we can do as curators or as artists is to show a few of its symptoms. So I did not follow a thematic approach. I had an interest in exposing the "unrepresentable" Europe. For me, it is the real challenge in the debates about Europe to accept this and to start right from this with our considerations.

İstanbul

Since the first concept for *Europe (to the power of) n* was written, Turkey has been on its agenda. Its potential entry into the European Union has been a controversial issue for years due to the Cyprus dispute, human rights, Islam, and religious as well as cultural questions. Discussing whether Turkey shares European values ignores the fact that the country already participates in some prominent European associations, such as the Union of European Football Associations, the European Broadcasting Union, the Council of Europe, the European Trade Union Federation. The question of whether Turkey belongs to Europe is further twisted when taking into consideration that many Turkish people already live in the midst of the EU. (In Germany, descendants of Turkish guest workers form the largest ethnic minority.) İstanbul was chosen, because it extends onto both the European and the Asian sides of the Bosphorus and holds its geopolitical and economic significance since the ancient world. The city's identity has changed over the centuries: it was the capital of the Eastern Roman and later of the Ottoman Empire. The official name was changed to İstanbul in 1930 and Ankara has been the capital of Turkey since 1923.

http://www.ibb.gov.tr/en-US/

SALT

MEASURE

BANU CENNETOĞLU
The List, 2012

Measure is a project that consists of two components: a public intervention by Banu Cennetoğlu and two films by Isaac Julien, which both talk about and question European borders. The economic crisis that has been setting the tone in world affairs for the past half decade has had extensive social and political consequences. The rise of right-wing politics and policies and an escalation in discrimination against immigrants is chief among them. This, however, is not a new issue, especially not in Europe. Even at the advent of the EU project, the idea of the European citizen came with its definitive counterpart, the other, which had already been formed through a colonial history. The borders drawn by the Schengen Convention delineate these identities rather than territories, regulating the movement of people.

The movement of people around the EU border has been a contentious issue in Turkey's accession process, as the EU expects systematic efforts to fortify their border from Turkey while it remains outside of it. In 2012, the EU agency Frontex signed a memorandum with Ankara stating the "establishment of practical cooperation between Frontex and Turkish authorities competent in border management". Having signed the 1951 Geneva Convention with geographical limitations, Turkey (being one of three countries who has done so) has legally only been granting refugee status to "foreigners" from Europe. While keeping this limitation in place, recently there has also been a bill proposed to the Grand National Assembly to regulate "foreigners" from Turkey's eastern borders as well.

In 1993, the year the Maastricht Treaty was signed, philosopher Étienne Balibar wrote that "the theorist who attempts to define what a border is, is in danger of going around in circles, as the very representation of the border is the precondition for any definition." *Measure* deals with this aporia and Banu Cennetoğlu cuts through it by publicly disseminating *The List*, a document that contains the names of more than 16,264 known refugees and asylum seekers who have died within or on the borders of Europe since 1993 (the document was last updated on 13 June 2012). It is compiled and updated every year by the Amsterdam based organisation UNITED for Intercultural Action.

List of 16264 documented refugee deaths through Fortress Europe

Documentation on 13-06-2012 by UNITED
UNITED for Intercultural Action, European network against nationalism, racism, fascism and in support of migrants and refugees
Postbus 413 NL-1000 AK Amsterdam phone +31-20-6834778, fax 31-20-6834582, info@unitedagainstracism.org, www.unitedagainstracism.org

found dead	number	name	country of origin	cause of death	source
26/05/12	20	N.N.	unknown	drowned, after an inflatable dinghy on way to Italy started to deflate off the coast of Lybia	Migreurop/LRP
19/05/12	5	N.N.	Anjouan Island, Comoros	drowned, after boat of 43 migrants sank off the coast of Mayotte (F)	Le Monde/AFP/Migreurop
19/05/12	15	N.N.	Anjouan Island, Comoros	missing, after boat of 43 migrants sank off the coast of Mayotte (F)	Le Monde/AFP/Migreurop
02/05/12	1	N.N. (16, boy)	Afghanistan	stowaway, suffocated in a truck into which he had hidden to avoid the border police checks	Migreurop/PICUM/AdnK/MP
01/05/12	7	N.N.	Somalia	died in a boat during a week-long voyage from LY to Malta, boat came ashore at Riviera Bay	UNHCR
29/04/12	3	N.N.	unknown	died in car accident while trying to escape a FRONTEX control, 2 migrants and the smuggler	Migreurop/KTG/TF1/PICUM/Clandestina/Age
28/04/12	1	N.N. (boy)	Egypt	drowned, after being thrown off a boat of 80 by smugglers when a patrol boat approached	Migreurop/LRP
26/04/12	1	N.N. (40, man)	Afghanistan	drowned, after being thrown overboard by smugglers dozens of meters from Calabria's coast	LR/Migreurop/PUCUM/FE
12/04/12	1	Alain Hatungimana (man)	Burundi	suicide, killed himself in the Netherlands in fear of being deported with his two children	DutchN/Migreurop/RNW/PICUM/ENAR
29/03/12	1	N.N.	unknown	body found in an advanced state of decay in the rural area of Tichero, Evros Prefecture (GR)	PICUM/Age/Clandestina
17/03/12	1	N.N. (±28)	unknown	drowned while trying to cross Evros River to enter GR, body found in area of Nea Vissa	PICUM/Age
16/03/12	5	N.N.	unknown	bodies found in boat of 57 on way to Lampedusa (I) rescued by Italian auth. in Lybian waters	PICUM/LR
15/03/12	1	N.N.	unknown	drowned while trying to cross Evros River to enter GR, body found near river in area of Soufli	PICUM
12/03/12	1	N.N. (28, man)	Eritrea	rolled over by the truck he tried to hide under to leave Greece, near the new port in Patras	PICUM/patrasT
29/02/12	1	N.N. (man)	Egypt	died of hypothermia, body found in a warehouse in the area of Korinthia (GR)	PICUM/Proto
21/02/12	1	N.N. (±20, woman)	Africa	died of hypothermia while trying to leave TR via Evros River, body found near Orestiada (GR)	PICUM/Infomob/Skai/Clandestina
21/02/12	1	N.N.	Sub-Saharan Africa	drowned while trying to enter Ceuta (E) by swimming along the coast from Morocco	MUGAK
21/02/12	1	N.N. (±23, woman)	Africa	body found by border guards in the Evros River (GR)	MNS
10/02/12	1	N.N. (±40)	unknown	died of hypothermia while trying to cross Evros River to enter GR, body found near Tichero	PICUM/Rizo
07/02/12	1	N.N. (25)	unknown	died of hypothermia in Health Centre of Soufli after crossing Evros River to enter Greece	PICUM/Skai
07/02/12	3	N.N. (±20)	Afghanistan	stowaway, suffocated on an Italy-bound truck and abandoned by smugglers near Parga (GR)	MNS
06/02/12	3	N.N. (±20)	Afghanistan	stowaway, died of asphyxiation in truck on way to Igoumenitsa (GR), a port leading to Italy	PICUM/TVXS
29/01/12	1	N.N. (29, man)	Iran	suicide, found hanged in asylum seekers house in Wurzburg (D), was in cure for depression	HRS/SD/MainP/U4IB/SOS/Karawane
25/01/12	15	N.N.	Somalia	drowned, after their vessel of 55 migrants sank, bodies found off the coast of Misrata (LY)	MNS
25/01/12	40	N.N.	Somalia	missing, after their vessel of 55 migrants sank off the coast of Misrata (LY)	MNS
22/01/12	1	N.N. (±25, man)	North Africa	body found floating in an advanced state of decomposition 7 miles from Cabo de Palos (E)	MUGAK/Verdad
15/01/12	15	N.N. (12women; 2men; 1baby)	Somalia	bodies found on Libyan beaches after shipwreck of boat part of 4 boats group on way to I	PICUM/FE/TimesM/AFP/jW
15/01/12	1	N.N.	Somalia	found dead alone in shipwrecked boat that was part of group of 4 boats on way from LY to I	PICUM/FE/TimesM/AFP/jW
15/01/12	40	N.N.	unknown	missing after shipwreck of a boat part of a group of 4 boats on the way from LY to I	PICUM/FE/TimesM/AFP/jW
12/01/12	2	N.N.	Afghanistan	missing after 2 plastic boats trying to cross the border GR-TR via the Evros River overturned	PICUM/ClandestinE/Infomob/TK
12/01/12	4	N.N.	Bangladesh	missing after 2 plastic boats trying to cross the border GR-TR via the Evros River overturned	PICUM/ClandestinE/Infomob/TK
10/01/12	1	N.N. (man)	unknown	drowned trying to swim ashore with life jacket, body found floating 33 miles from Motril (E)	MUGAK/ElDia
08/01/12	1	N.N. (±28, man)	Sub-Saharan Africa	drowned trying to swim ashore with a life-belt, body found on the beach in Melilla (E)	MUGAK/LV
05/01/12	1	N.N. (21, man)	Guinea-Conraki	reportedly lack of medical help after asked for assistance in Barcelona's detention centre (E)	IRR/MUGAK/LV/18Des/EP/EPress
03/01/12	1	N.N. (young man)	Afghanistan	died from smoke inhalation from fire lit in tin can to keep warm inside abandoned truck (GR)	MNS
01/01/12	1	N.N.	Palestine	died of hypothermia trying to cross the river Evros between GR and TR, part of group of 15	CMau/KI
01/01/12	2	N.N. (9, girl; 55, man)	Afghanistan	missing after they tried to cross the river Evros between GR and TR, part of a group of 15	CMau/KI
27/12/11	1	N.N. (12, boy)	Iran	died of hypothermia, body found by the police along the shores of the Evros River (GR)	MNS
27/12/11	1	N.N. (59, woman)	Iran	died of hypothermia, body found by the police along the shores of the Evros River (GR)	MNS
27/12/11	1	N.N. (±30, man)	Africa	died of hypothermia, body found by the police along the shores of the Evros River (GR)	MNS
19/12/11	1	N.N. (41, woman)	Congo	died of meningitis hours after her admission to hospital from Aluche detention centre (E)	IRR/ICARE/MUGAK
10/12/11	2	N.N.	unknown	bodies found in the area of Petalo (GR), tried to cross the border TR-GR via the Evros River	MNS
06/12/11	1	N.N. (±32, man)	North Africa	reportedly smugglers tortured and then shot him, found outside Thriassio Hospital,Attik (GR)	MNS
06/12/11	2	N.N.	Somalia	died at sea on way from Libya in a boat of 44 migrants found 75 miles south of Malta	TimesM
01/12/11	1	N.N. (16, boy)	Syria	killed after a car chase in Evros (GR), involving Greek border police and FRONTEX officials	MNS
in Dec 11	11	N.N. (men)	Algeria	missing after they sailed from Sidi Lakhdar (DZ) in the direction of Spain on a makeshift boat	FE/Le MatinDZ
28/11/11	1	N.N. (±25, man)	Sub-Saharan Africa	drowned, found in port of Ceuta (E) in advanced state of decomposition	FE/ElDia/MUGAK
27/11/11	3	N.N.	Afghanistan/Pakistan	bodies found in the south-eastern port of Brindisi (I) after a vessel sank off the nearby coast	MNS
27/11/11	20	N.N.	Afghanistan/Pakistan	missing after a vessel sank off the coast of Brindisi (I)	MNS
26/11/11	30	N.N.	Afghanistan/Kurdistan/Sri	feared drowned, missing after boat sank off Brindisi coasts (I) on the way from Turkey	FE/LR/PICUM/LRB/Blitz/MUGAK/Raz/ABC/V
26/11/11	3	N.N.	unknown	drowned, bodies found afer boat sank off Brindisi coasts (I) on the way from Turkey	FE/LR/PICUM/LRB/Blitz/MUGAK/Raz/ABC/V
23/11/11	3	N.N.	Sub-Saharan Africa	drowned, bodies found on Moroccan beach, part of group of 90 who tried to swim to Ceuta	MNS
09/11/11	43	N.N.	unknown	missing after contacting Italian authorities because their boat was taking water in rough seas	MNS
11/10/11	2	N.N.	Iran	died in accident, smugglers' car overturned as they tried to avoid a police road block	MNS
07/10/11	2	N.N.	unknown	died instantly after being run over by train near Feres (GR) while walking along the railway	MNS
in Oct 11	1	Khaled Khodena (man)	Iraq	murdered due to his religious after deportation from Sweden, his asylum claim was rejected	UNHCR/Sveriges
in Oct 11	1	Michael Kelly (man)	Liberia	found dead in his room at the Gerstungen asylum seekers centre (D) 10 days after he died	VRF
28/09/11	4	N.N.	Tunisia	burned, fire caused by lit candle in Pantin squat, Paris (F) - a municipality owned building	MNS/FTRC/Raz/Le Monde/Libération
28/09/11	2	N.N.	Egypt	asphyxiation, fire started by lit candle in Pantin squat, Paris(F)- a municipality owned building	MNS/FTRC/Raz/Le Monde/Libération
14/09/11	1	N.N.	unknown	drowned, pushed off jetski when smuggler saw coastguards approaching in Andalusia (E)	Sur/Mugak
24/08/11	1	N.N. (man)	unknown	murdered, shot by Frontex officer while shooting at boats crossing TR-GR border, Evros river	ClandestinE/Son Dakika/MNS
04/08/11	100	N.N.	Africa	unknown, bodies thrown overboard from LY boat rescued 104 miles from Lampedusa (I)	Telegraph
02/08/11	1	N.N. (man)	Asia	suicide, hanged himself in a shower at Campsfield House Immigration Removal Centre (GB)	MNS
01/08/11	25	N.N. (men)	Sub-Saharan Africa	suffocated, travelling on boat with 275 survivors, SOS sent 35 miles from Lampedusa (I)	SP/FE/Le Figaro
29/07/11	30	N.N.	unknown	unknown, bodies found on boat, engine failed after leaving Alexandria (Egypt) 1 week before	FE/Libero
13/07/11	1	N.N. (23, man)	Cuba	stowaway, crushed to death, found in the wheel-bay of an Iberia passenger plane in Spain	MNS
05/07/11	1	N.N. (25-30, man)	Maghreb	drowned, body found near Selinunte, Trapani (I) in advanced state of decomposition	ANSA/FE
01/07/11	1	N.N. (man)	Sub-Saharan Africa	died of hypothermia trying to swim ashore with life jacket, body found off Ceuta's coast (E)	MNS
29/06/11	1	N.N. (man)	Sub-Saharan Africa	suspected hypothermia, body found wearing life jacket in "Three Stones", Ceuta (E)	FE/VDG
25/06/11	45	N.N.	Morocco	feared drowned, fell from a boat found neat Motril, Granada (E), 2nd boat still missing	FE/PICUM/Diario de Navarra
25/06/11	1	N.N. (20, man)	Morocco	drowned, body found 4 miles from capsized boat in Motril coast, Granada (E)	FE/PICUM/Diario de Navarra
25/06/11	1	N.N. (38, man)	Ghana	epileptic seizure, Libyan refugee on boat from Lampedusa(I) to mainland, was known sufferer	PICUM/FE/AdnK
03/06/11	1	N.N (30, woman)	Nigeria	found dead in police cell, was detained for having no papers in Zurich airport (CH)	Migreurop/AP
02/06/11	270	N.N.	West Africa/Pakistan/Bang	drowned, 2 found, overcrowded boat capsized 300km from Tripoli (LY) to Lampedusa (I)	Migreurop/Mugak/UNHCR/Reu/Universo/Gua
01/06/11	1	N.N.	unknown	unknown manner of death, died on the way from Libya to Malta body thrown overboard	ANSA/Fe
29/05/11	3	N.N.	unknown	survivors reported bodies missing while reaching the coasts off Sant'Antioco (I) from Libya	ANSA/FE
29/05/11	4	N.N.	unknown	drowned, bodies missing, boat collided with other boat off Libya's shore on the way to Italy	FE/ilClandestino
22/05/11	1	N.N. (woman)	Sub-Saharan Africa	drowned, decomposed body found by Cabo de Gata (E), probably from 5/5/11 shipwreck	ABC/Mugak
08/05/11	1	N.N. (30, man)	unknown	stowaway, died of overheating in truck carrying cablewheels in Fulda (D) travelling from GR	HessenR/HNA/Welt/SP
08/05/11	1	N.N. (20-25, man)	unknown	stowaway, died of overheating in truck carrying cablewheels in Fulda (D) travelling from GR	HessenR/HNA/Welt/SP
06/05/11	45	N.N.	Sub-Saharan Africa	drowned, 13 found, 32 missing, boat of 600 sank off coasts near Tripoli (LY) on the way to I	LR
06/05/11	3	N.N. (babies)	Sub-Saharan Africa	drowned after boat of 600 sank off the coasts near to Tripoli (LY) on the way to I	LR
05/05/11	22	N.N. (men)	Sub-Saharan Africa	feared drowned, boat sank 2 miles from Adra, Almeria coast (E), 29 survivors	Humano/Publico/MUGAK/EP

Deaths are listed if they can be put down to "Fortress Europe"
(border militarisation, asylum laws, accommodation, detention policy, deportations, carrier sanctions...)

In collaboration with curators and institutions, Cennetoğlu has shown up-to-date and translated versions of *The List* in several countries since 2006, using public display structures such as advertising boards and newspaper supplements. The database format of the document, as made available by UNITED on their website, is not altered, simply blown up. Presented to passers-by in this way, the work functions as an interruption or intervention in public space rather than providing any theoretical context or definition of the border issue and its corresponding violence.

As part of *Measure*, *The List*, 2012, appeared in İstanbul between 15 and 23 October on outdoor advertising boards, as well as on poster boards in the Metro, which carries 230,000 people daily. As it is proposed here, however, *The List* is not merely meant as a socio-political project, but also as a long-term process in exploring the borders and the scope of artistic practice. Facilitating the display of such a document is a delicate and hazardous task, especially when the artist and her related context are the facilitators. Would it be more legitimate and thus more efficient if such an intervention were executed by an NGO? What happens if a "responsible" act ends up being a mere spectacle? Do responsible acts differ according to their contexts? These questions were tackled in a conversation between Cennetoğlu and Emel Kurma of the Helsinki Citizens Assembly at the Walk-in-Cinema at SALT Beyoğlu on 19 October 2012.

During the first installment in March 2007, *The List* was displayed throughout the city of Amsterdam. A sixteen-page list was translated to Greek and distributed as a supplement in the daily paper on 28 September 2007. And finally, from 31 January to 8 February 2011, the thirty-six-page document was on display in seventy-two locations in Basel-Stadt and in Baselland.

This indoor component was followed by
two films, also shown in the Walk-in-Cinema at
SALT Beyoğlu, in which Isaac Julien evokes
borders through historical, theoretical, practical,
performative, and poetic means. In *Peau noire,
Masque blanc*, 1996, a documentary-style film
that narrates the story of the life of Frantz Fanon,
the Algerian anti-colonialist writer, Julien takes
on a colonial history that may be read as
both a constitutive element and a mirror of the
predicament of the EU borders today. In a later
short film, *WESTERN UNION: Small Boats,* 2007,
Julien traces journeys on the Mediterranean,
depicting the European shore as the space
where the joyous beach is juxtaposed with a stray,
red T-shirt, a material as well as symbolic trace of
those lost at sea. Together, these two works
span a historical period from colonial Europe to
the European Union, delineating their borders.

Cennetoğlu's intervention and Julien's films
encircle the European border in ways that go
beyond theorisation or representation, rendering
it barely visible through its violence rather than
its material existence. The fact that this project
is taking place in İstanbul, Turkey – which poses
as a border not only to the EU but also to the
Middle East – will conceivably open it to further
readings from diverse perspectives.

Artists:
Banu Cennetoğlu, Isaac Julien

Claudia Hahn-Raabe, Goethe-Institut İstanbul

The *Measure* programme as part of the *Europe
(to the power of) n* project consisted of Banu Cenntoğlu's
project *The List,* 2012, a conversation between the
artist and Emel Kurma of the Helsinki Citizens
Assembly, the screening of two films by Isaac Julien,
and an artist talk given by Julien. The first component
of the project, *The List,* appeared in İstanbul on
fourty-nine outdoor advertising boards, as well as
poster boards in the Metro line. The screenings and
talks were held at SALT Beyoğlu. This programme,
which was scattered through space and time aimed at
engaging various audiences in unexpected ways
drawing attention to the consequences of the EU and
the state's policies concerning refugees and asylum
seekers. The project came at a time when the circumstances and news surrounding the refugee and asylum
seekers status and rights in Turkey was in flux after
having received 150,000 refugees from Syria within the
past year, which crystallised an already existing
phenomenon. The interest in and coverage of the project reflected its importance within this conjecture
as well as within the artworld's engagement with
such social issues.

ISAAC JULIEN
Frantz Fanon: Black Skin White Mask, 1996
(film still)

ISAAC JULIEN
Cast No Shadow (Western Union
Series No.1), 2007

CARRYING EUROPE AROUND

Barbara Steiner

Within the frame of *Europe (to the power of) n,* ideas about Europe are set in relation to one another re-evaluating what Europe could be. Evidently, Europe means something else in the United Kingdom than in Poland, Serbia, Belgium, Belarus, Turkey, or in the Basque Region – not to forget about China, the most distant point of the project.[1] In no case can the importance of Europe be taken for granted anymore – neither from an "insider's perspective" nor from a non-European perspective. Looking into recent debates about a European Union that committed itself to solidarity towards its members, the idea of a unified Europe seems to become a burden and a nuisance instead. The question *"Does Europe no longer matter?"*[2] frequents people's thoughts increasingly, be it from an inside or a more distant point of view. In terms of the locations that are part of *Europe (to the power of) n,* the views on Europe slightly differ but are not enthusiastic: in Belarus Europe remains fairly vague. It is widely seen with ambivalence between affection and animosity that is deepened by pro-Russia and pro-Europe promoters in the country. In Serbia, Europe and the EU oscillate between acceptance and refusal, depending also on whether one feels closer to the Ottoman or the Austrian-Hungarian past. In Poland, the tendency towards Europe and the EU can be described as pessimistic. Nevertheless, this goes along with a general tone of pessimism considered by many to be a cultural *dispositif.*[3] In the United Kingdom, Europe as a project driven by a joint idea hardly matters and the EU is often seen negatively, nourished time and again by considerations of leaving the union.[4] In Belgium, Europe is both manifest, when seen against the EU's institutions and concrete policy in Brussels, and quite often rhetorical, when seen in the light of conjuring common European agendas. Turkey is veering away from Europe and the vague promises of the EU towards other allies, and China preferably does not deal with "Europe" as a whole but with single states.

The locations within *Europe (to the power of) n* not only play an important role in terms of variety and contextual differences: they also challenge conceptions of a powerful united Europe from various perspectives. Some either distance themselves from such a conception from a unified Europe from the very beginning – the distance the United Kingdom has to the European Union and to continental Europe is quite legendary – some place great emphasis on political independence or autonomy, as it is the case in Norway, Poland, or the Basque Region which extends over France and Spain. Some are viewed with suspicion or even excluded by those who already see themselves as part of a European community. Turkey, Belarus, and Serbia seem to raise this kind of suspicion. Regarding Belgium: its local

1   How Europe is looked at varies, although tendencies in the interpretations can be noticed, which are very often connected to (older or more recent) national narratives and their relationship to the larger construct Europe. Certainly, and this goes without saying, it is also important to take into consideration that within each country quite a number of rivalling ideas about Europe and the EU can be found, too.

2   Referring to a speech by US Secretary of Defence Robert Gates; Richard N. Haass, president of the Council on Foreign Relations, wrote in the Washington Post on 17 June, that in the coming decades Europe's influence on affairs beyond its borders will be limited, and it is in other regions, not Europe, that the 21st century will be most clearly forged and defined. Richard N. Haass, "Why Europe no longer matters", 17 June 2011 http://articles.washingtonpost.com/2011-06-17/opinions/35266108_1_common-defense-policy-european-allies-nato, 22 December 2012. Chinadaily picked up the topic on 20 June 2011 http://usa.chinadaily.com.cn/opinion/2011-06/20/content_12765714.htm

3   The project by Janek Simon shown at the Muzeum Sztuki in Łódź was explicitly dedicated to the idea of pessimism as a significant cultural feature, which precisely aimed at testing "Polish pessimism" within a highly optimistic surrounding. Joanna Sokołowska/Jarosław Lubiak, Janek Simon, in *Untimely Stories*, exhibition catalogue, Muzeum Sztuki, Łódź, p.168.

4   *The Economist's* cover of the issue from 8 December 2012: "Goodbye Europe What would happen if Britain left the EU" dedicated its main subject to Europe. Volume 405, London, 2011.

political and social ruptures, the conflicting parties of the Walloons and the Flemings, and the fact that Brussels is a centre of EU politics, which tries to keep up common agenda, makes it an interesting choice for *Europe (to the power of) n*. However, not only national narratives, self-perception, and attributed perception matter in the project, the inherent contradictions at work in the particular cities, respectively the contradictions in relation to their wider context, were decisive for the project. London was chosen as the polyglot home of many people from all over the world, as a leading global city (despite all acclaimed Britishness), and İstanbul – situated on two continents – because of its role as the crossroads of European civilisation, which is nourished by cultural influences from Asia Minor. Novi Sad, located in the Vojvodina, was selected, because it is the administrative centre of a small region in Serbia, where more than twenty-six ethnic groups live together, although facing a constant conflict with nationalists who try to defend ethnic purity whatever the price. Łódź, once leading in the textile industry, was chosen because of its massive triple transformation from capitalism to socialism and back, and from once being very cosmopolitan at the centre of attention, to being peripheral now. Minsk was selected as the centre of the "last European dictator's"[5] representational power and contrasted with Vilnius, where the exiled European Humanities University is located.[6] Oslo was taken, because it is one of the fastest growing capitals in Europe. It is home to many migrant workers from non-European countries, which contribute to and participate in the wealth of the city.[7] Donostia – San Sebastián is known as a popular seaside resort in the Basque Country, both open to the world – due to shipping (in the past) and tourism (today) – and rooted to the soil when connected to Basque agendas. And Brussels was chosen because of its ambiguity towards Europe and the European Union: it benefits a lot from the EU's institutions but Europhobia can also be found in the heart of the European Union.

When the choice of locations for *Europe (to the power of) n* were made, the emphasis was never placed on completeness, but on challenging ideas of a powerful exclusive European community from peripheral positions – even if some locations are centres in other respects, such as London or Brussels. Thus, "peripheral" does not refer to a geo-graphical location or the bounds of affluence here, but to the fragile relationship of these cities (and countries) with a self-identifying "core" Europe. The term "periphery" appears most appro-priate to explain this phenomenon: it describes an outer defining line (of a district, or a town), originally meaning "carrying around" or "circulation". This circular movement – i.e. the pro-ductive and constructive "carrying around" of Europe – formed the starting point of *Europe (to the power of) n* and of reflections on what Europe could be if there were no central authority or strictly predefined core.

5   Alexander Grigoryevich Lukashenko has been serving as the President of Belarus since 1994. Under Lukashenko's rule, the govern-ment's conduct has been globally denounced for being out of line with international law and human rights. Former and current European and American leaders have called Belarus "the last true remaining dictatorship in the heart of Europe". "Rice: Russia's future linked to democracy", cnn.com, 20 April 2005 http://edition.cnn.com/2005/WORLD/europe/04/20/rice.dougherty/index.html

6   The European Humanities University (EHU) is a private, non-profit arts university founded in Minsk in 1992. Celebrating its 20th anni-versary in 2012, EHU has been headquartered in Vilnius, Lithuania, since authorities expelled it from Belarus in 2004. http://www.ehu.lt

7   The actual location is Høvikodden near Oslo. Høvikodden was chosen because of the Henie-Onstad Kunstsenter, founded by the famous Norwegian ice-skater Sonia Henie and her husband, who were aiming to connect national and international art, local and avant-garde movements. Today the art centre is dealing critically not only with its history, but also with its current role within an increasingly global world, connecting local and global agendas.

As a point of departure, thirty scenarios and thus thirty ways of thinking about Europe from the perspective of art were developed in 2011 and early 2012. Within the *Europe^n* eleven scenarios were exchanged among the project's participants between July 2012 and April 2013.

The following section presents this exchange.

EXCHANGING SCENARIOS
EXCHANGING IDEAS

Nils Norman's, *Updated Social Composition of Romney Marsh*, 2011/12,

was introduced by Kit Hammonds in *Scenarios about Europe 1* and extended to a triptych with the same title in Hammond's exhibition *The Europa Triangle* in London. Later it was shown in Filip Luyckx's exhibition *Cultural Freedom in Europe* in Brussels.

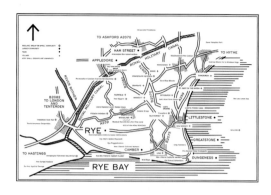

Kit Hammonds, London

The original commission of Nils Norman's work was intended to frame an aspect of the show within a speculative fiction. Nils Norman's speculative map shows the area of Romney Marsh in South-East England and imagines the social groups that may emerge under anarchy. It is a region of lowlands whose landscape has a particular, desolate character. Among Romney Marsh's landmarks is the nature reserve of Dungeness, which houses a nuclear power plant. The Marshes have a long history of independence and rebellion having been the starting point for the Peasant's Revolt in 1381, which ultimately failed, but nevertheless marks one of the earliest popular uprisings against serfdom in Europe. In 1840, Thomas Ingoldsby declared the region a fifth continent, due to its desolate landscape and its separatist spirit. More recently, a vehement local campaign arose around the construction of a wind farm that attracted an unlikely group of activists drawn from an unlikely mix of middle-class residents who insisted that the turbines would visually destroy the unique landscape. Accused of "Eco-Nimbyism" and of being a pawn of the pro-nuclear lobby, the grass-roots protest group challenged the accepted wisdom that wind farms provide a genuinely renewable form of energy production and, to some extent, split the environmental lobby.

Norman's map depicts an evolution of local groups where the political left and right and social identities have become cross-pollinated. Some of the groups are based on past or current movements, while others suggest new hybrids. Norman's work has long employed fiction, albeit carefully researched, drawing on social movements and incidences of radicalism. The stories told through his work reflect on how such ideas might exist in contemporary life through a satirical lens that allows for a dystopic present to emerge from utopian ideals of the past. In the triptych of diagrams produced for *The Europa Triangle,* Norman suggests a group of radicals occupying a specific, real building under the proposals of 17th-century French thinker Charles Fourier. This contemporary phalanstery is situated within a real, suburban, and, therefore, conservative "middle England", but in a region with a strong history of its independence.

Filip Luyckx, Brussels

Nils Norman conceives maps with an alternative political economy. They show potential societies that are beneath the existing ones. Most of them look utopian at first, but they do not deny a sense of irony. So, maybe even utopists cannot believe in fundamental changes anymore? Norman's work gets to the point, which is important for the Brussels exhibition: that Europe is a mixture of ideas, lifestyles and experiments, requiring at least some degree of tolerance in order to survive.

Charting the exchanges of works of art and participants that took place

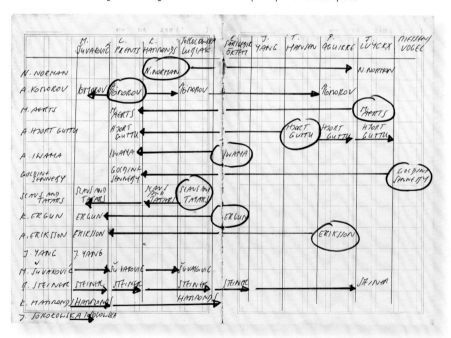

92

Aleksander Komarov's film *Language Lessons,* 2011,

was introduced by Lena Prents for *Scenarios about Europe 2.* **A new film** *Палiпадуацэнне (Palipaduazennije),* 2012, **which connected to the first one, was produced and shown at the launch of** *Europe (to the power of) n* **at the Haus der Kulturen der Welt in Berlin for the first time. Later, Komarov took** *Language Lessons* **as the super title of two films and related projects. Both films were shown in the exhibitions** *West of East* **in Minsk,** *Untimely Stories* **in Łódź,** *Asymmetric Europe* **in Novi Sad, and** *Constellation Europa* **in Donostia – San Sebastián.**

Lena Prents, Minsk

Impassioned discussions about the language of the country are held in Belarus between representatives of two concepts of language, which are reflected on intensively: the old concept understands language as a base for national identity and more modern ideas interpret language as a construct. Russian was once language of the Belarusian modernisation from 1918 until the late 1980s. During the early perestroika years, Belarusian became a form of resistance. In the new Law About Languages, it was fixed as an official state language. But only five years later, the law was changed and both Belarusian and Russian have been indexed as state languages. Nowadays, using one or the other language can be considered as a sign of a certain position: from resistance to lifestyle, from nationalism to cosmopolitanism. This historical context and the present struggles are the background for Aleksander Komarov's film *Language Lessons.* The film recounts the legend surrounding the foundation of the city of Minsk and introduces the view of Belarusian intellectuals who reflect on the national language. *Палiпадуацэнне (Palipaduazennije)* developed from this film project. Komarov continued with his research on language as an idea that does not necessarily separate people, but which could develop a potential for breaking new ground.

Jarosław Lubiak and Joanna Sokołowska, Łódź

The film *Palipaduazennije* is an attempt to find another language to express oneself with. Aleksander Komarov takes his point of departure from an observed distinction between native and national tongues and the consequences of this difference for individual identity as it struggles to remain in confrontation with the experience of emigration. The relation between uprootedness and rootedness – referring to op-posite phenomena, which nevertheless remain in close symmetry with each other – is a key issue that this project confronts.

The artist invited members of the Belarusian community in Rotterdam to a meeting devoted to language. The meeting took place at the city's botanical garden, which houses plants from various climate zones around the world, thus constituting a genuinely artificial environment that produces near-native conditions for flora from distant countries. The artist conducted an experimental lesson with the participants. First, he asked them to select words related to the experience of being an immigrant. The participants were then invited to a recording studio where they recorded their chosen word in a Belarusian translation. However, as none of the participants were fluent in the language, they could not be sure whether their pronunciation was correct. This uncertainty provoked a game in which the participants combined Latin plant names with Belarusian words. Overcoming two foreign languages with an artificial one, allowed them to find another form of expression. Significantly, such a possibility could not have been provided by any natural language, as they found the moment of rootedness only when creating a language that could not be fully understood by anyone else. The artificiality of the situation in which the immigrants find themselves and which they discuss during the meeting is reflected in the artificiality of the language created to express and name it. The experiment suggests that this artificiality cannot be described with words found in any natural language, because the latter stems from a deep-rootedness in a traditional community. It demonstrates, at the same time, that the experience of the unfamiliar requires creating an artificial language in which it could be expressed. This language, in turn, can be best translated into the equally artificial language of contemporary art. It is in the work of art, such as Komarov's film, that exotic words find their natural environment, just like the exotic plants in the artificial climatic conditions of a botanical garden.

The exhibition *Untimely Stories* was an attempt to create an environment in which various, often conflicting languages as well as singular or local experiences could meet through art. Alongside Wendelien van Oldenborgh's installation *Supposing I Love You. And You Also Love Me,* Komarov's work became a form of translation, searching for relations between the dissimilar and the unique and stimulating resonances where differences encounter resistance, limit, or suppression.

Miško Šuvaković, Novi Sad

In *Asymmetric Europe,* Aleksander Komarov's film *Палiпадуацэнне (Palipaduazennije)* was shown in the exhibition's film programme. Komarov is an artist who explores conditions of and resistances to forms of communication in Belarusian and European society. His explorations seek to index and cinematically document the consequences of the divergences between the native and the national languages in diasporic conditions. Using metaphors of enrooting and uprooting, he highlights the relations that exist in a diasporic community's original language as well as its current one. The artist invited Belarusians living in Rotterdam to a meeting about language. The meeting took place in a botanical garden, which housed plants from different climate zones. The artist asked his interlocutors to pick words they might relate to their experiences of emigration and then reduce their selections to just one word each. The participants were then taken to a studio, where their chosen words were translated into Belarusian. They were unsure whether they were pronouncing the words correctly. This turned into a game in which the participants combined the Latin names of plants with Belarusian words. The film shows an entirely constructed social situation that takes place between different languages and their slippages vis-à-vis the national identity of the speakers and the cultural context of emigration. Language is marked as an important means of communication as well as of cultural identification in all of its instability and variable exoticness of pronunciation, meaning, and mediated sense. Komarov's anthropology of linguistic expression makes visible a particular problem. For me, his work was yet another critical asymmetry in European modalities of living among different cultures, i.e. cultures of origins and cultures of settling. It is an anthropology of a fragile contemporaneity between here and there.

Peio Aguirre, Donostia – San Sebastián

Aleksander Komarov's work is striking for its narrative sensibility and the complexity of its content. Both works, *Language Lessons* and *Palipaduazennije,* pertain to the documentary genre, however, neither of the films is pure documentary. They benefit from the qualities of art on the verge of film, documentary, and the written essay. Asked how the meaning of the films has changed according to their respective context, I would say their context is less relevant, because they connect specific issues with universal ones. From the beginning, both films were fundamental for my exhibition. They are shown together in a special screening programme and they are translated and subtitled both in Basque and Spanish. The issue of language and multi linguistic societies has become one of the main lines of thought in my project. It corresponds with our local situation – that of a bilingual society, in which one of the languages spoken dominates the other (Spanish over Basque), and in which negotiations between the two cannot be entered without conflict. Aleksander Komarov's voice speaks from the diaspora (as a Belarusian artist who lives in Berlin) and also about diaspora (Belarusian people in Europe). This approach, which is also rooted in his own experiences, makes his work an important contribution to the discussion about exclusion and inclusion as well as to the shaping of national identities, historical memory, and more. The issue of identity expressed through language is very decisive in the Basque context and therefore shared with themes explored in Komarov's work. This is why his participation is essential to the project.

Mobile Monument Performance, 2012, by Michaël Aerts

was introduced by Filip Luyckx in *Scenarios about Europe 3,* and was later shown with partly different elements in the exhibition *West of East* curated by Lena Prents in Minsk. Parts of the work were also presented in Filip Luyckx's exhibition *Cultural Freedom in Europe* in Brussels.

Filip Luyckx, Brussels

Michaël Aerts's sculptures are conceived as nomadic works composed of hybrid cultural elements. This implies shifts in content and use. All the participants are given the opportunity to build up a monument. Although the issue is less about the sculpture finding a position and more about the shift that can take place from the participant's individual backgrounds to a common ground of mutual understanding. Despite all sorts of personal differences the participants might have – largely due to the fragmentation of society as a whole – people in general have to achieve agreement on elementary rules. In the Brussels exhibition, one obelisk stands next to its flight case, another one is installed on a trolley; they are potentially movable. However, this time they are not taken by volunteers throughout the city, as it happened in other places, because the exhibition context of the Economic and Social Committee does not allow an easy access and least of all movement of works into or out of the building. Nevertheless, Aerts's work references the constitutive role of monuments in creating strong visual identities all over Europe. Within the context of the European capital and administration it seems to be only logical that the monuments are standing still for a while.

Lena Prents, Minsk

For Michaël Aerts a monument is a symbol of transience. Meanings and interpretations are subject to permanent change. The further back in history the erection of a monument lies, the more diffuse the original intention behind it becomes. Due to its strong physical presence, the purpose of a monument in public space is to pay homage to an event or a person over the course of centuries, although this is often forgotten over the course of years. A monument is degraded to become part of the fixtures and fittings of a town. The inhabitants of the town remain largely unaware of the original reasons and meaning behind the decision to erect it. It was this point in Aerts's thinking which led him to construct a mobile obelisk that became a visual signifier. The transformable obelisk in the exhibition space was only a few metres away from the monument at Victory Square, whose monuments also take the form of an obelisk. Its purpose it is to remind us of the victory of the Belarusian people in the Great Patriotic War. However, these parallels occurred only to a small number of visitors. The historiography of heroism is a given thing that is not called into question. Monuments for heroes primarily fulfill the purpose of providing landmarks within the space of the town. Aerts's performance communicated the associations he makes between the cult of monuments and the role of communities. Furthermore, the only people who dared to create a new monument from the mobile obelisks, which could easily be taken apart, were children – as long as their parents did not coerce them into behaving in an appropriate, orderly fashion inside the exhibition room.

Ane Hjort Guttu's *Freedom Requires Free People,* 2011,

was introduced by Tone Hansen in *Scenarios about Europe 2* and shown in the exhibitions *West of East* by Lena Prents in Minsk, *Cultural Freedom in Europe* by Filip Luyckx in Brussels, and *Constellation Europa* in Donostia – San Sebastián by Peio Aguirre.

Tone Hansen, Høvikodden / Oslo

The film *Freedom Requires Free People* depicts a school system rooted in egalitarian, humanist ideals and situated in a social democratic political system in one of the world's richest countries. At the same time, however, the Scandinavian school system is moving rapidly towards European standardisation and an even greater emphasis on results.

Freedom Requires Free People presents an eight-year-old boy, who has what one might call an anti-authoritarian attitude, an almost irrepressible need to question and challenge existing rules. The film is an attempt to understand what motivates him and to show him as an example of someone who, almost by nature, thinks critically. His striving represents the freedom struggles going on everywhere, every day, affecting common people in their schools, workplaces, and communities as well as institutions, which, even if they are not particularly destructive, are still perceived as oppressive by those who engage with them.

Lena Prents, Minsk

Ane Hjort Guttu took a very definite stance in her film *Freedom Requires Free People*. The artist stated that she was not concerned with making a contribution to the subject of the portrayal of childhood in contemporary art, but with commenting on the rigid and disciplinary school system, which trains, shapes, and forms the individual. This context was certainly understood by the visitors to the exhibition in Belarus, but it was not a dominating aspect of the discussions that ensued. These were mostly concerned with the interplay between the boy, who is the main protagonist of the film, and the artist. Was he manipulated by the filmmaker? Did he adapt his behaviour according to her directions? Whilst some people believed they had found evidence of this in the film itself, others insisted on making a comparison: there are more and more difficult, nonconformist children around. They should be shown and the approaches of the people who portray them should be confronted. At the centre of the discussions was the question how such special children are treated in the family, in society, and in the media.

Peio Aguirre, Donostia – San Sebastián

The screening of *Freedom Requires Free People,* which is about a boy who has his own opinion concerning school and is quite resistant to forms of education imposed on him, is featured alongside a chapter of the TV series *Ante, 1975,* (Arvid Skauge and Nils Utsi) and an excerpt from *Lära för livet / Learning for life, 1977,* (Carin Mannheimer). The main idea in this programme is to address the subject of school and education and to introduce to the public in San Sebastián certain examples from Scandinavian contexts. From the Basque perspective, Nordic social democracy has always been viewed as being idealistic and, at the same time, has served as an aspiration. The screening programme allows us to confront established clichés as well as to open up toward reflections about various social models. Historically, Spain has been behind in comparison to other European countries. Since the end of the 1970s, this has changed completely. Nowadays, school enrolment starts at a very early stage for children (from the age of two years) and different models of schools and education are heavily debated – above all in the Basque context due to the complexity of linguistic policies and bilingualism. Parents have to choose the language for their children paired with the ideological connotations this choice carries along. I have selected one chapter of the 1970 TV series *Ante*, which features an eight-year-old Sami boy who refuses to attend school in Norway, because it shows that the struggle for identity begins already at school age. Seen against the background of the local situation, this has been a major issue in the Basque country due to the difficult balance between the dominant (Spanish) and the minor (Basque) idiom, to which the integration of the progeny of immigrants and the introduction of a third language, English, must be added as well. Education is a very hot topic in Spain at this moment, not only because of the economic crisis and the associated budget cuts, but also due to the recent reactionary educational reform launched by the Spanish right-wing government that threatens to reduce the existing consensus based on plurality and intends to merge the various national and regional cultural traditions into one nation state with a single national identity.

Filip Luyckx, Brussels

Education can be seen as the main influence on life and as a basic condition (or obstacle) for critical learning. Ane Hjort Guttu's film *Freedom Requires Free People* shows the conflict between human intuition, human nature and of learned behaviour. Freedom means here, last but not least, that individuals are able to develop their abilities and talents according to a humane society. However, psychological conditioning could push people to follow patterns of imposed behaviour in opposition to this ideal.

Asako Iwama's *Where we Cook and Eat Together,* 2011,

was introduced by Esra Sarigedik Öktem in *Scenarios about Europe 2*. On the occasion of the launch of *Europe (to the power of) n,* Iwama's *she knows only what he knows that she knows, he knows only what she knows that he knows* was shown at Haus der Kulturen der Welt in Berlin. A variant of this was realised in the exhibition *West of East* by Lena Prents in Minsk.

Esra Sarigedik Öktem, İstanbul

Where we Cook and Eat Together, developed in collaboration with Asako Iwama, dealt with the condition of being "foreign" and "exotic" and questioned the female position within both Turkey and Japan respectively and within a host European culture. It brought into view and subverted cultural stereotypes and clichés through a culinary exchange.

The initial idea for *Where we Cook and Eat Together* was derived from a recipe for plum marmalade. While researching various plum marmalades, their ingredients, and their taste, my interest was drawn to the "translation" process of this marmalade, as it was carried out in various locations. On occasion of the Leipzig presentation, a cabinet was displayed inside the museum to hold the marmalades and other preserves the project participants contributed for the duration of the scenario presentation. The material shown was basically the outcome of a somewhat nomadic practice. The archival aspect of the cabinet also alludes to a state of flux since it is filled and emptied over time. It seems, therefore, that the scenario can go anywhere, including my hometown İstanbul. Borders and cultural differences exist everywhere within and around communities, countries, and political unions such as the EU.

Lena Prents, Minsk

Asako Iwama's performance in Minsk was entitled *she knows only what he knows that she knows, he knows only what she knows that he knows*. Iwama invited a male actor to take part, who was found by following her instructions: "somebody who wants to be me, a thirty-six-year-old Asian female, Japanese artist, who performs cooking for a one-day event. Should be a man. Do not mind what age or biological sex, could be gay or transsexual, but somebody who defines himself as Male." In this way, the performance in Minsk began long before it was staged in Gallery ў. The artist bought the ingredients at the local market, which she then cooked with the help of her assistant. For the main part, however, she held a conversation with this person, who had been a complete stranger to her up until this point, lending him her ego. The serving of the Japanese rice balls and all communication with the public was carried out by Iwama's alter ego. Afterwards, Roman Romanovich said that the most difficult moment was when he was addressed by a Japanese person in Japanese.

I invited Iwama to Minsk, because during *Scenarios about Europe* I had noticed how intensely she analyses a given situation, how precisely she works. In her artistic practice she can carefully show, explain, and define every individual step in the working process – in an intellectual, distanced way, but also on an emotional and personal level. Iwama's medium is food. Sensual experience is an important component of her performances, but it is not the only one. The artist wishes to bring into the open everything that is associated with food as a cultural activity: forms of communication, working roles, and relationships between the sexes. The experience of foreignness and individuality can be constructed via food. For the exhibition in Minsk, which was concerned with the relationship between Eastern and Western Europe and with Belarus in the middle, I found Iwama's formulation of questions around the non-European context extremely interesting. In Belarus, one rarely comes into contact with this kind of influence: there is not a large number of immigrants from outside Europe. The theme of migrated identities is perceived in a one-sided way, with a strong migration of artists away from

Belarus. This increasingly leads to discussions on the topic of the true Belarusian identity. For Iwama, a Japanese person living in Germany where she works within an international team and frequently travels around the world, the concept of identity must really be a transient one. During the performance, she lends her identity to another person – a man, who is by now no longer a complete stranger to her – thus pointing towards the conditional nature of patterns, rituals, and contexts. The artist discloses the paradox inherent in the idea of an identity: it is always diffuse and incomplete, yet it is still seen as a unity and we strive towards it. In a place where discussions on identity played an important role, Iwama's performance was a welcome source of irritation.

Goldin+Senneby's (with Swedish County Administrative Boards) *Not Approved: Field Inspection Photographs of Rejected Landscape Features,* 2009–2011, and *Shifting Ground,* 2009,

were introduced by Markus Miessen and Felix Vogel* in *Scenarios about Europe 1* and shown in the exhibition *West of East* by Lena Prents in Minsk.

* Markus Miessen and Felix Vogel were appointed curators for London until the beginning of 2012, and part of the *Scenarios about Europe* project in Leipzig.

Markus Miessen and Felix Vogel, London

Constituting almost half of the EU's budget, agricultural subsidies have long been infamous for their production of excess: mountains of butter and lakes of wine. Today the grounds are shifting. A new agricultural paradigm has taken form in which subsidies have been decoupled from production. Farmers no longer receive support to overproduction, but to reinvent themselves as environmental entrepreneurs and guardians of the landscape. They are no longer required to provide food, but to provide open fields.

The work consists of thirty-two photographs taken by Swedish bureaucrats in order to evaluate whether the landscape elements meet the EU subsidy standards. This is a selection of landscapes that did not meet those standards. *Not Approved: Field Inspection Photographs of Rejected Landscape Features* leads on from a previous Goldin+Senneby production, *Shifting Ground* from 2009. In *Shifting Ground,* Goldin+Senneby commissioned the political speechwriter Simon Lancaster to write a speech exploring issues of agriculture, bureau-

cracy, subsidies, and space/landscape and drawing parallels, amongst other things, between agricultural funding and arts funding.

Lena Prents, Minsk

In the exhibition *West of East* in Minsk, *Not Approved: Field Inspection Photographs of Rejected Landscape Features* and *Shifting Ground* opened the section entitled "Economy". In a Belarusian context, it seemed important to me to point out the dominance of economic conditions, on which culture and art are also dependent. In Belarus, the work of Goldin+Senneby would have reinforced the most vehement critics of the European Community in their feelings of resentment against the EU. The agricultural policy of the EU as presented by Goldin+Senneby gives many people strong cause to doubt the integrity of EU bureaucracy. At the same time, one could assume that the circumstances described have nothing to do with the supposedly prospering conditions on the island of Belarus. Already, dubious concepts of the entertainment industry are no longer discussed in a serious way, but actually put into practice in agriculture as well as in town development. The economisation of the field of art is also progressing rapidly at the same time as it is being created. Several visitors asked whether the cover of

Shifting Ground was an original, or whether I had commissioned it especially for the exhibition in Minsk: the motifs featuring climbing plants, ears of corn, and little leaves, so folkloric and homely, somehow seemed to suit Belarus.

The speech in *Shifting Ground,* "to be delivered by an actor", was written by a speechwriter. It is an integral part of Goldin+Senneby's work and their artistic approach. For me, it was quite clear that it should be translated. As soon as the translation was finished, colleagues in Belarus immediately suggested staging it as a performance – as it had been when the work was first presented in Stockholm. The performance, staged by the director Tatiana Artimovich and the actor Vitaliy Kravchenko, made a considerable contribution as far as art mediation was concerned, for the contents could not be fully grasped by the visitor until he or she had become involved with the formal level. Framed photographs of unspectacular landscapes accompanied by a brochure – in spite of explanations and descriptions – made an aloof, unapproachable impression on those visiting the exhibition. "European" was the description some of them used.

Slavs and Tatars's *Reverse Joy,* 2012, which is a part of the cycle *The Faculty of Substitution*,

was introduced by Jarosław Lubiak and Joanna Sokołowska in *Scenarios about Europe 3* and later shown in their exhibition *Untimely Stories* in Łódź, in which it was extended by *Weeping Window,* 2012, which is part of *Friendship of Nations: Polish Shi'ite Showbiz.* Another work of Slavs and Tatars, *Triangulation (Not Moscow, Not Mecca),* 2012, was exhibited in *The Europa Triangle* curated by Kit Hammonds. As part of *Asymmetric Europe* in Novi Sad, Slavs and Tatars were invited by Miško Šuvaković to give their lecture performance *Chains We Can Believe In,* 2012.

Jarosław Lubiak and Joanna Sokołowska, Łódź

Weeping Window and *Reverse Joy* are part of ongoing projects through which Slavs and Tatars reflect on the relation between Catholic culture in Poland and Shia culture in Iran, and more generally between European and Islamic cultures. What they are proposing, within a project aimed at reinventing Europe through art, is a different attitude towards the past and history, and different ways of remembering or experiencing them. Slavs and Tatars discover latent relations, often manifested in reversals between distant and seemingly unconnected cultures. Sometimes they accompany their discoveries with fictitious constructions disguised as academic discourses.

Both projects hark back to the Shia celebrations of the month of Muharram. On the tenth of that month in 680 CE, Hussein ibn Ali, the grandson of the Prophet Muhammad, was killed by Shimr ibn thil-Jawshan ibn Rabiah al Kalbi, commander of the Ummayad army, during the Battle of Karbala. The event marked the beginning of the schism between Shia and Sunni Muslims. Every year, Shia Muslims all over the world celebrate a public holiday to mourn the fact that they could not participate in the battle and die for Hussein. In Iran, these celebrations assume the form of a ten-day-long festival. Despite the intense mourning going on there, Slavs and Tatars note, the rituals are filled with a tangible sense of satisfaction, even joy. Public space, often highly restricted in countries such as Iran, suddenly livens up with the atmosphere of a street party.

Weeping Window is a transmutation of the Iranian custom of painting invocations to the relatives of the Prophet Muhammad on the rear windows of cars. Here, an inscription in honour of Hussein has been replaced with the words "Khhhhhhhajda Khhhhhhhłopaki" written on the rear window of the Polski Fiat 125p, a Polish equivalent of the Iranian-made Paykan.

Reverse Joy refers to the Muharram custom of dyeing water in fountains crimson-red to make it look like blood, but the red fountain in Łódź may also serve as an allusion to the Polish cult of martyrdom and the blood spilt over the centuries by Poland's countless veterans. Both works, therefore, are about the relation between the Polish and Iranian cultures, a relation as real as it is imaginary.

Kit Hammonds, London

Some artists' practices are peculiar blind spots until someone forces them into your vision. Slavs and Tatars have been within the same orbit as me for some time, however, I was surprisingly unaware of their broader practice until being put in touch with them through the third scenario by Joanna Sokołowska and Jarosław Lubiak. It was only through Payam Sharifi's lecture performance that the theme of triangulation matched precisely in that moment with my own thoughts around which I was thinking I might structure the exhibition in London. Seen through Slavs and Tatars's practice Europe can be pictured not as a centre, but as a negative

"in between", influenced by what is going on around it politically, spiritually, and ideologically. In thinking about how to rethink Europe, their position offered a productive conversation with my own, and a key to resolving it. After such an influence, it was only natural that they should continue to be part of the exhibition's progression.

Miško Šuvaković, Novi Sad

Slavs and Tatars presented an installation and a lecture perform-ance previously selected by the two Polish curators Joanna Sokołowska and Jarosław Lubiak for *Scenarios about Europe* in Leipzig. For *Asymmetric Europe*, Slavs and Tatars performed their lecture *Chains We Can Believe In* over Skype. It revolved around the curious story of a Sufi mosque in the middle of New York; the Russian avant-garde poet Velimir Khlebnikov, whose nickname was "the Russian Dervish"; and anti-modernist and minimalist artist Dan Flavin. This complex and eclectic story points to numerous moments of contact and tangled states between the Western and the Eastern, that is, the Euro-American and the Eurasian cultures; to traces of life between Islam, Christianity, and pragmatic materialism, that is, obsessions with big and peripheral modernisms.

In their performances, installations, and publications, Slavs and Tatars highlight the relative relationship between centre and periphery, semi-periphery, and para-centre. Their work pro-vokes religious asymmetries, cultural asymmetries, political asymmetries, and certainly unstable positioning of contemporary subjectivity vis-à-vis the global world and its visible and invisible hierarchies. In the context of the exhibition in Novi Sad, the group's lecture was extremely significant due to its reference to the Borromean rings of the East and West of civilisation, which are important for the historical character of Serbia's contemporary society, since it historically owes its hybrid identity to the Ottoman as well as to the Austro-Hungarian Empire. By working on different fragments of the historical heritage of the vast area east of the Berlin Wall and west of the Great Wall of China, Slavs and Tatars, entirely unrelated to Serbia, generated an unexpected and pro-blematic homology to Serbian culture in its unstable positioning in the east of the West and the west of the East.

Köken Ergun's *Binibining Promised Land,* 2009–2010,

was introduced by Esra Sarigedik Öktem in *Scenarios about Europe 3* and later shown in Miško Šuvaković's exhibition *Asymmetric Europe* in Novi Sad, together with *Ashura*, 2012, another film by Köken Ergun.

Esra Sarigedik Öktem, İstanbul
Part of my third scenario was Köken Ergun's *Binibining Promised Land,* 2009–2010, a video work that revolves around a beauty pageant of and by the Filipino migrant community in Israel. Beauty contests are very popular among Filipinos both at home and abroad. "Binibining Filipinas", established in 1964, is the most important beauty pageant in the Philippines. The Filipino community in Tel Aviv created their own beauty pageant in a nightclub inside the Tachana Merkazit and named it "Binibining Filipinas Israel". Although Ergun's film engages with the immigrant experience from a non-European perspective, its depiction of the sense of being a stranger and the dynamics of hierarchy and subordination that come with it resonate ubiquitously.

The life of the Filipino community in Israel resonates within the context of İstanbul in the familiarity of the way in which these migrant women live and work. In Turkey, where one of the primary areas

of work for immigrants, especially women, is in the caregiving and housework sector, Ergun's insightful observation of a similar transnational community finds a diverse yet much ignored context. That is not to say, however, that appreciating this work, not only in my hometown, but also in the artist's, suggests such a direct reading of it.

Miško Šuvaković, Novi Sad
Köken Ergun's films *Ashura*, 2012, and *Binibining Promised Land*, 2009–2010, were shown in the exhibition *Asymmetric Europe* at the Museum of Contemporary Art of Vojvodina in Novi Sad. Ergun is an artist, whose films perform critical reconstructions of anthropological documents about contemporary global life and its media representations. For instance, in *Binibining Promised Land* Ergun shows us the weekend entertainment of Filipino workers, who are temporarily residing and working in Tel Aviv, Israel. They live in poor conditions in the neighbourhood surrounding the central coach terminal of *Tachana*

Merkazit. On the Sabbath, that is, on Saturdays, there are no coach services. On those days, foreign guest workers visit the terminal's modernist building and pass the time in its shops: a place where these temporary residents of Israel "socialise" together. They also stage their famous beauty pageants. The central event, "Binibining Filipinas Israel", is organised in a nightclub. Ergun's film is a documentary exploration of the modifications that Filipino customs of entertainment have undergone in Israel. The documentary film material is a sample of the cultural mapping of forms of life under conditions and circumstances of transition.

The topic of *Ashura* is the marking of the eponymous Muslim religious holiday in a local community within a suburb of İstanbul. In the year 680 CE, according to the Islamic calendar, the Prophet Muhammad's grandson, Imam Hussain, was martyred in the Battle of Karbala. Shiite Muslims all over the world commemorate his death on the tenth day of the month of Muharram. The Caferi community in the Halkalı district of İstanbul organises a ceremony every year that attracts thousands of people. Amongst Turkey's predominantly Sunni Muslims, the event is known mostly for its ascetic and sometimes bloody rituals. Many people, and especially the media, come to see the dramatic performances and the crying women with headscarves who participate in the Ashura. In his films, Ergun explores the politics and poetics of contemporary rituals, focusing on the performative aspects of these ceremonies to investigate the contradictions and transitions of Middle Eastern cultural identity in global times.

Annika Eriksson's *Wir bleiben / The Last Tenants*, 2011,

was introduced by Peio Aguirre in *Scenarios about Europe 2* and shown, newly edited, in his exhibition *Constellation Europa* in Donostia – San Sebastián. Prior to this, Miško Šuvaković presented Eriksson's first edit in his exhibition *Asymmetric Europe* in Novi Sad.

Peio Aguirre, Donostia – San Sebastián

Over the last two decades, Swedish artist Annika Eriksson has developed a multifaceted body of work, in which she criticises various manifestations of commodity mainly through portraying situations that witness the unavoidable presence of institutional and economic power and class structures. Her work *Wir bleiben / The Last Tenants* deals with how European cities have changed through the effects of an ever-increasing economisation. In this case, the focus is on Berlin Mitte, an area which has been rapidly commercialised. It can be seen as an example of how the free flow of capital can quickly and irrevocably change lives, neighbourhoods, and entire cities. This process has happened rapidly in Berlin, but it can also be observed in other European cities. Actually, the work exposes how capitalism is an agent of change that needs to be constantly in circulation for its own regeneration. People move, they go from one place to another and finally from one country to another. Displacement and transformation are, therefore, the main issues of Eriksson's film, which portrays with sensitivity the witnesses of this change. The artist interviewed her former neighbours who had to move out of their home, in which they had lived for generations. Eriksson's film serves to map a phenomenon that is global and, as with any study of capitalism, it shows that it is not enough to focus on an individual problem at a certain time or place, but that these problems are connected on a large scale. The work was originally shown as part of *Scenarios about Europe* at the Museum of Contemporary Art in Leipzig. At that time, it emphasised Berlin and Germany's history within the construction of an idea of Europe and within the configuration of the European Union. Its presentation in San Sebastián coincided with a highly sensitive moment in the current economic crisis in Spain, which is another example of a crisis in the Eurozone that the European Central Bank and the leading political members are not able to settle. With 500 families being evicted in Spain every day, foreclosures have become a source of great suffering. Among those families there are also some who resist.

Miško Šuvaković, Novi Sad

Annika Eriksson is a Swedish artist working in Berlin. In *Asymmetric Europe,* her film *Wir bleiben / The Last Tenants,* 2011, was shown in the exhibition's film section. In her work, Eriksson has addressed the performativity of documentary material since the 1990s. Her work sets up provocative relations between film scripts and "real life scripts". *Wir bleiben / The Last Tenants* is about a building in the central Berlin borough of Mitte, where the artist has lived for a number of years. The building was erected in 1755 and over the course of its 250-year history underwent numerous transformations. Eriksson's video portrays the building's last four tenants. When the announcement came that the building would be redeveloped for another purpose, it was evacuated. The last four tenants decided to stay put until the end. The building's story is one about a transitional Europe and more specifically about its transformations from the Cold War to the development of the European Union. It is a story about survival, habitation, persistence, and disappearance.

Annika Eriksson was important for the Novi Sad project as an artist working inside Europe, unlike Ergun and Yang who work at or beyond the borders of Europe. Her work presented an opportunity to confront internal and external asymmetries of those European forms of life that are in permanent transition. This film draws attention to the problem of being in a permanent "state of emergency", making it further significant for us who look towards Europe from a permanent state of emergency and the turbulences of the former East and the Balkans. The film is about understanding a situation marked by instability, potential displacement, and transformation.

Jun Yang's *Paris Syndrome,* 2007–2008,

was shown on occasion of *Asymmetric Europe* in Novi Sad. Miško Šuvaković invited Yang who participates in *Europe (to the power of) n* as curator of the Chinese part in his artistic capacity.

Miško Šuvaković, Novi Sad

Jun Yang's film *Paris Syndrome*, 2007–2008, was selected and presented in the film section of the exhibition *Asymmetric Europe* at the Museum of Contemporary Art of Vojvodina. *Paris Syndrome* was chosen as an example of an intercultural dialogue between European and Chinese articulations of everyday life through forms of architecture in transition. The term "Paris syndrome" denotes a psychological disorder typically diagnosed in Japanese workers and tourists living in or visiting Paris. The trauma occurs when a Japanese visitor confronts, for the first time, the reality of Paris and cannot reconcile his fantasies about the city with the often hostile reality of the metropolis. It can be described as a negative cultural shock. In his video work of the same name, Jun Yang explores and presents simulations of clichés of aspiration, of a desired reality, and realisations of one's life ambitions. The video was shot in the new residential districts of Guangzhou, which emulate the iconography, form, and atmosphere of European upper-middle-class neighbourhoods. The film shows couples, lost and absent amidst a fantasy of affluence come true.

Yang is an artist who problematises the complexities and fragile inconsistencies of Sino-European encounters, mutual recognitions, exchanges of urban identities, the visibility of everyday forms of life, and ways of inscribing the Other into the self. In his works, however, one cannot tell who the self is, or who the Other is, whether the self is Chinese and the Other is European, or vice versa. This relativisation of the process of identification is rather important in that Yang produces Europe's asymmetries in relation to China's. In the context of *Asymmetric Europe,* his work matters because it shows the complexity of positioning and indexing European relations.

L'INTERIEUR

Høvikodden /Oslo

The project *Europe (to the power of) n* was in fact carried out in Høvikodden near Oslo, the location of the Henie-Onstad Kunstsenter, founded in 1968. Today, the multidisciplinary art centre places emphasis on its role within an increasingly global world linking local and global agendas. From Oslo to Høvikodden it is approximately a fifteen-minute drive; bus trips take about twenty-five minutes. In the context of *Europe (to the power of) n*, this was as important as the fact that it is located in the greater area of Oslo – the cultural, economic, and governmental centre of Norway. Oslo has held its status as one of the world's most expensive cities, and the fastest growing European capital in one of the wealthiest countries in the world, due to oil and gas that have been discovered in the North Sea and the Norwegian Sea. A large portion of this growth stems from immigration, mainly from non-European countries. In the context of debates about Europe and the European Union, Norway's policy can be seen as ambiguous: The country participates in the European Union's single market via the European Economic Area (EEA) agreement and contributes financially, although without wanting to be a member of the European Union. Referendums in 1972 and 1994 indicated that the Norwegian people wished to remain outside the European Community and later the European Union.

http://www.oslo.kommune.no/english/

LEARNING FOR LIFE

HENIE-ONSTAD KUNSTSENTER

DARCY LANGE
Studies of Three Birmingham Schools, 1976
(installation view)

Læretrfor
livet

Læring for Life, 2012
Catalogue design by Eriksen / Brown

SERVET KOÇYIĞIT
Higher Education, 2006
(installation view)

107

I've nearly got it.

JOOST CONIJN
Siddieqa, Firdaus, Abdallah, Soelayman, Moestafa,
Hawwa, Dzoel-kifl, 2004
(installation view)

LEARNING FOR LIFE –

AN EXHIBITION FOR ANYONE WHO

HAS ATTENDED SCHOOL

What kind of citizens of the world of tomorrow are we producing with our current school system? What is the relationship between freedom and discipline in schools? Are we concerned solely with measurable results through EU regulations such as the PISA test or national tests to be compared with other countries, or should school be nurturing free individuals? If the latter, what role could art play in the process? *Learning for Life* spanned the period from around 1900 to the present in the form of works newly commissioned for the exhibition, historical objects from the Oslo School Museum, and material loaned from archives. Significant films and TV series were also included. The exhibits ranged from a painting by Edvard Munch to films by Abbas Kiarostami and Erik Løchen.

The exhibition looked at the role of the primary school in society through the works of art. Central to the exhibition was Ane Hjort Guttu's film *Freedom Requires Free People*, which raises questions about the place of the individual in school. The exhibition also interweaved cultural history with artistic themes allowing us to pose questions such as: what technical skills did society need at the time when the elementary public school system was first being established? On the other hand, what skills and knowledge does contemporary society expect its future citizens will need? The exhibition took place both in the main hall (Storsalen) and in HOK LAB, while parts of the children's workshop facility had been incorporated into the exhibition.

In conjunction with *Learning for Life*, the Henie-Onstad Kunstsenter developed a special programme for the HOK junior workshops in collaboration with the school of photography at Kulturskolen. Every Sunday the workshops moved into the exhibition space with a project named after Nils Christie's book *Hvis skolen ikke fantes (If School Did Not Exist)*. Throughout the exhibition period, children and teenagers worked on a large collective mural on the western platform; the theme was the troubling but challenging idea of a world without school as we know it today. The exhibition was also presented as part of *Cultural Rucksack* (a national scheme for professional art and culture in schools in Norway) where tenth-grade pupils spent a day in the exhibition and discussed their everyday life in schools.

The interdisciplinary seminar *Hva er det vi vil med barna? (What Do We Want for Our Children?)*, which took place in February 2013, was aimed particularly at teachers, artists, educationalists, and art historians. A reader of commissioned and already published texts, artworks, and reports was launched in spring, published in collaboration with Sternberg and co-edited by Lars Bang Larsen.

Sections of *Learning for Life* will be exhibited at Tensta konsthall in Stockholm and subsequently to other institutions.

Artists:
Jeannette Christensen, Joost Conijn, Harrell Fletcher / Ella Aandal, Priscila Fernandes, Ane Hjort Guttu, Luis Jacob, Abbas Kiarostami, Servet Koçyiğit, Darcy Lange, Erik Løchen, Line Løkken, Carin Mannheimer, Edvard Munch, Palle Nielsen, Øystein Wyller Odden, Allan Sekula, Arvid Skauge / Nils Utsi, Kjartan Slettemark, Peter Tillberg

YOU CAN ALWAYS JUST LEAVE SCHOOL

AND GO ON SOCIAL SECURITY[1]

The only time I feel free is when I get out of school and go to the stable. I'm free when I'm with my horse.

I think we have a great time at school. We have nothing to complain about!

Comments by schoolchildren who saw the exhibition Lære for Livet (Learning for Life)

Ellen Marie Fodstad

In November and December 2012, the Henie-Onstad Kunstsenter invited schoolchildren to visit the exhibition *Learning for Life*. Instead of a traditional guided tour about different styles of art, artists, or materials, we based the visit to the Art Centre on a discussion about education and freedom, which revolved around a few selected works from the exhibition. The works chosen were: Ane Hjort Guttu's *Freedom Requires Free People,* Servet Kocyigit's *Higher Education,* Jeanette Christensen's *The Philosopher's Stone,* Edvard Munch's *History,* Harrell Fletcher's / Ella Aandal's *What Are We Doing on Monday,* Peter Tillberg's *Will You Be Profitable, Little One?,* Palle Nielsen's *Model for a Qualitative Society,* and Line Løkken's *Sandaker Secondary School.*

These works were picked as being good springboards for discussion. We asked questions about how far the schoolchildren were able to influence their own everyday life. When did they feel free during the day?

1 The title of this essay is taken from a comment made by a schoolchild who visited the exhibition *Learning for Life.*

How does school shape them? What is the experience of being at school like? Which decisions are possible for them to influence, should they want to? Many of the children were frustrated about how little influence they have on their own daily lives. For example, several of them felt that the pupil's council was merely a formality: "they never listen to our suggestions anyway; in any case, they never do anything about them. They just say 'yes, perhaps', and nothing more happens. We are never allowed to decide anything, whatever our suggestions might be about." We also asked questions about all the written and unwritten rules they have to abide by. Most of the children had posters with rules at school, telling them how to behave. Did they think these posters were necessary? Would they have behaved differently if the posters were not there? Most of the pupils felt that it was right to have the rules visible at school. As one of them said: "You get so frustrated by all the rules telling us not to run in the corridors, not to go to the toilet more than once before lunch, and to turn off our mobile. But we wouldn't necessarily be any better off without rules. Anarchy and chaos are not freedom either." At the same time, some of the schoolchildren asked whether it was equally important to follow all the rules: "When you just follow the rules without thinking for yourself, you are like a sheep following the flock. Do you really have to follow all the rules all the time?" In the words of one boy: "The only 'must' in life is that we are all going to die, otherwise it's all about 'can'!" Some of the other children protested at this and pointed out that when you break rules, it has consequences for others. How exactly? "It becomes difficult to concentrate and we don't learn as much!"

The pupils in the top class of middle school who visited the Henie-Onstad Kunstsenter are about to take what is perhaps the first big decision of their lives – they must choose which secondary school they are to attend, which will influence their future. Did they think that they were given a free choice? "No, it's quite stressful; the school you go to says something about who you are. If you break rules, get bad marks and are absent a lot, it can influence your future. You won't get into the school you want and other people will regard you as a loser."

So how will it be in the future – do you have more freedom when you get older? Most of the schoolchildren cried "YES!" Why? "I think we become freer as we get older, but at the same time, what we do has larger consequences. You get a job, mortgage, house and children, and a lot more responsibilities." What kind of consequences did the pupils believe it could have if you just leave school and live on social security? "You always have a kind of choice anyway, even though that choice is not always the best one for your future."

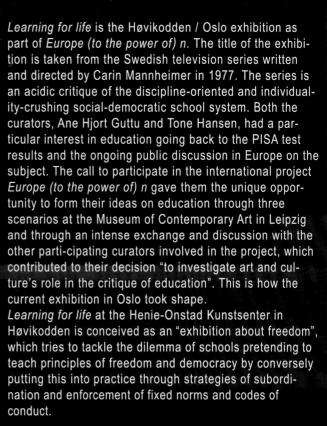

Ane Hjort Guttu
Freedom Requires Free People, 2012
(installation view)

Kristiane Zappel, Goethe-Institut Oslo

Learning for life is the Høvikodden / Oslo exhibition as part of *Europe (to the power of) n*. The title of the exhibition is taken from the Swedish television series written and directed by Carin Mannheimer in 1977. The series is an acidic critique of the discipline-oriented and individuality-crushing social-democratic school system. Both the curators, Ane Hjort Guttu and Tone Hansen, had a particular interest in education going back to the PISA test results and the ongoing public discussion in Europe on the subject. The call to participate in the international project *Europe (to the power of) n* gave them the unique opportunity to form their ideas on education through three scenarios at the Museum of Contemporary Art in Leipzig and through an intense exchange and discussion with the other parti-cipating curators involved in the project, which contributed to their decision "to investigate art and culture's role in the critique of education". This is how the current exhibition in Oslo took shape.
Learning for life at the Henie-Onstad Kunstsenter in Høvikodden is conceived as an "exhibition about freedom", which tries to tackle the dilemma of schools pretending to teach principles of freedom and democracy by conversely putting this into practice through strategies of subordination and enforcement of fixed norms and codes of conduct.

The exhibition is certainly about freedom, but much more about education with its disciplinary tools, about order, about exaggerated principles of functionality: of school architecture and spaces, of the arrangement of objects in the class room, of education goals, of the individual itself. *Will you be profitable, little friend?* is the gruesome title of Peter Tillberg's painting from 1972 and it seems that this has not changed, when today in Europe and elsewhere the students' performance continues to be above all the most prevailing criteria with which the qualities of educational systems are measured.

The particular relevance of the project focusing on education is quite obvious in a country like Norway where the PISA ranking from 2006 has slipped significantly below the OECD average. Although, according to UNESCO, Norway's school system achieves a high standard with respect to the inclusion of all students disregarding their individual capacities. However, this creates a lot of pressure for the students to adapt to that inclusive system. Students with behaviour deviating from what is considered normal will encounter difficulties. That is the subject of Ane Hjort Guttu's impressive documentary film *Freedom Requires Free People*, 2012, about eight-year-old Jens who strongly rejects the rules and regulations of his school as it restricts his personal freedom and liberties through the learning process.

Around 700 people came to the opening of the exhibition, and in the six weeks following the opening around 3000 school children visited the exhibition and saw the film about Jens. Tone Hansen observes: "They all sit down in the auditorium and see it from beginning to end and then they see the exhibition while discussing the film. It is the best educational situation we have had so far. I think everyone can relate to the protagonist's fight against being formed without having a say. He dares to say what many think. This also goes for adults: it is a film not only about a boy and his problems, but about the child's outspoken project – that of criticising authority and making authority visible."

And that might become a turning point or at least a point of discussion: listen to the children, respect individuality and resistance to the norm as is practiced through art, and in the works presented as part of the exhibition.

ERIK LØCHEN
Citizens of Tomorrow:
A Film About Oslo's Public Schools, 1950

PETER TILLBERG
Will You Be Profitable,
Little Friend?, 1972

Oslo School Museum
Students's work, handwriting, 1900
(installation view and detail)

Oslo School Museum
Students's works, needlework, 1920–1980

Single and common agendas

Barbara Steiner

Each of the curators of *Europe (to the power of) n* was given "carte blanche" in how to approach Europe, how to translate possible European agendas into the particular contexts of the respective cities and countries, and how to bring local agendas into a European debate. However, there was one obligation for everybody: common formats and activities related to the project and its communication had to be considered and to be actively participated in. They provided the ground for an exchange among the participants and introduced *Europe (to the power of) n* as a joint project. Whereas the conferences primarily fostered an exchange among the contributors[1], the web project aimed to connect over and above to a general public. By using the meaning (semantics) of information, it gives associated information about venues, sites, projects, artworks, and people and offers, therefore, a comprehensive insight into *Europe (to the power of) n*. Over the course of the project, this multitude of information has grown further through its users and has been connected with other informational sources beyond the project's realm. Concerned with the interfaces between new technologies, their possibilities and social demands, the work of Konrad Abicht, Vanessa Boni, Andreja Hribernik, Christopher Köhler, and Tristan Schulze has entered a new territory in the field of mediation and communication of complex cultural projects.

The Europe^n Book – primarily based on images taken from the various locations – translates the narrative of *Europe (to the power of) n* into the printed format.[2] Both the web project and the *Europe n Book* look into the realisation and manifestation of *Europe (to the power of) n* and allow for multiple readings of the individual projects in relation to one another. Both built, so to speak, a common space, which is fictitious, because the single curatorial contributions never met or were seen together at one physical site; and real, because an actual space of exchange was created over the course of the project. The design of the *Europe n Book* is part of the overall visual identity of *Europe (to the power of) n* developed by Oliver Klimpel. Referring to the project's general agenda, which is based on multiple views and approaches, Klimpel examines the possibilities of design and its capacity of constructing identities, which are multifold themselves. The project's logo, which mutates, meanders, doubles, multiplies – or to put it differently, remains unstable and ambiguous – was offered to be appropriated by the partner institutions. Its character changed according to the surrounding and the decisions made by the designers of the partner institutions and resulted in a variety of printed matter and different scales of collaboration.[3]

A similar approach, that takes multifoldness into consideration, applies to the spatial concept conceived by Christian Teckert and Christine Bock: they proposed a virtual European exhibition space comprising all venues and evolving around three standardised elements: line, surface, and three-dimensional objects. At each venue, there was a line to be drawn at the height of one metre (benchmark line), the wall surface above the line was to be painted according to a fixed colour scheme (*The Guggenheim Colors by Fine Paints of Europe*), from which the curators could choose their favourite colour. And finally, three objects based on the standards of the euro-pallet – to be

1 The conferences were held in Berlin, Łódź, Høvikodden / Oslo, and London and were partly public. The conference in Berlin also had the function to introduce and to promote *Europe (to the power of) n*. It marked the start of the project, which afterwards continued in the cities involved. The conference in London completed the project and provided a reflection about its implications.

2 Its picture-driven character marks an important difference to the previous book, *Thinking Europe The Scenario-Book*, which was mainly text driven.

3 Some of the collaboration partners decided for the minimum use of Klimpel's visual sign, others invited him to extend his concept to the exhibition display and/or to take over the design of other printed matter (London, Novi Sad, Beijing).

variably used as shelve, display, wall, or stage – circulated among the participating institutions.[4] Every adaptation was photographed on site and mounted together on occasion of this book to create, again, a common virtual space that nevertheless remains fragmented. The contributions of both Teckert / Bock and Klimpel show that visual and spatial identity in regard to *Europe (to the power of) n* did not mean a strict, uniform canon of forms and spaces, but the appearence of a multitude of graphic and spatial possibilities. Nevertheless, even if the participants were given space for individual expression, they were at the same time subjected to restrictions and a given structure.

Common ground was also established through the exchange of the scenarios among the curators, which they had developed during the preparatory period in Leipzig. In total, eleven scenarios were reframed according to the respective contexts.[5] Most frequently shown was *Freedom Requires Free People* by Ane Hjort Guttu. In Norway, her film about an eight-year old boy, who fights against a disciplinary and standard-ising school system and claims the right of autonomous thinking, was intended to be a comment on school education, whereas in Belarus the film's meaning shifted to a reflection about manipulation, discussing whether the filmmaker had manipulated the child's behaviour. In Brussels, it raised questions of freedom and restrictions and how they can be balanced. In San Sebastián the emphasis was put on the ideological impact schools have on the individuals. This example demonstrates best that exchanging scenarios and reframing them led to shifts in perception and put on view the interrelation between the production of meaning and the context in which the scenarios / artworks were presented. It also showed the grown interests of the curators involved in having an exchange with colleagues and artists about the possibilities art has in debates about Europe.

There was one basic principle, which arised throughout the whole of the project: maintaining individual leeway and being able to develop certain ideas indepen-dently of others, but at the same time acting as part of a larger network and having to open up to the positions of others. The balance between self-centredness and relatedness was fragile on purpose. From the outset *Europe (to the power of) n* aimed to investigate existing antagonistic spaces that are political, economic, social, and cultural in nature. Within and through the project, a conceptual framework was provided that allowed the participants, the artistic director, the curators, the designers, the architects, and the institutions involved to reconsider their own attitudes in light of other attitudes, to articulate different approaches, and to seek out common ground, however temporary that might be.

4   The London curator Kit Hammonds, for example, encouraged his students to fill the shelves with their statements and research material. The Łódź curators, Jarosław Lubiak and Joanna Sokołowska, used the architectural elements for displaying information about the exhibition and the workshops connected to it. The Høvikodden / Oslo curator, Tone Hansen, used them for workshops with children. The Novi Sad curator, Miško Šuvaković, linked most elements with artworks in the exhibition and reserved one element for informative material about the project, something the Brussels curator, Filip Luychx, did as well. The Chinese curator, Jun Yang, asked Oliver Klimpel and Christian Teckert / Christine Bock to develop the entire spatial structure for his project at Vitamin Creative Space in Beijing. However, some curators did not make use of all three elements proposed by the architects. *The Guggenheim Colors* were only loosely applied in reference to the set of colours.

5   Besides the exchange of scenarios some curators lectured at the venues of their colleagues. The Chinese curator invited all curators involved in *Europe (to the power of) n* to participate in a conference and in an exhibition aiming to establish connections between people and institutions involved in the Europe project with potential partners in China / Taiwan.

Oliver Klimpel

Inserting a stimulating or disruptive unknown within the familiar might start constituting a renewed dialogue with one's own history and sense of belonging. In a dialogue in which we act and play out our propositions and messages, conventional graphic codes of identification are under permanent siege, yet present.

Just as attempts to grasp, define, and comprehend conclusively the graphic design response to the project, *Europe (to the power of) n* can be portrayed as a process of ongoing adjustments, where specific aspects are brought into focus, then lost in a blur again whilst adjusting to another aspect on the periphery. Never settling for one angle but demanding awareness anew and the desire to decipher the whole. What kind of qualities could graphic design for this project put challenge to?

To create a visual identity for an art project that is both non-representational and speculative, yet seeks to investigate through practice, is somewhat of a conundrum. It would have seemed a complete contradiction to create a conventional brand for a project that is characterised by a counter-authoritative principle of a defined set of unsynchronised viewpoints and voices. Its multiplicity surely betrayed the logic of a singular graphic language to make the parts identifiable to a wider audience. Or did it? And yet, participation and strategies of hyper-flexibility within the constructions of graphic identities are full of frivolous clichés.

DESIGNING A VISUAL IDENTITY FOR *EUROPE ^{n}*

A Currency of Contention

Dear participants and friends,

since the last time we saw each other and following the scenarios in Leipzig, the project has now been developing into new spaces and ideas, on the various locations.
    I would like to invite you to continue the conversation with me about its graphic formats and mediation and how your concepts can manifest themselves in your city and beyond. This is also a further elaboration and challenge to the idea of a corporate identity in the context of Europe and this project as my contribution to it.
    Nevertheless, to achieve some level of consistency throughout I have produced some elements, which I would like you to use for the umbrella identity of the project. In the following, a few notes about their use.

Looking forward to continuing our dialogue.
Best wishes,

    Oliver

A document, which outlined the use of the graphic elements, was sent out to all participants to invite them to collaborate on the design.

The poster-edition by Oliver Klimpel consists of a range of prints
made using the split fountain printing technique. They include four
designs called "Flags", which feature gradients and represent the
increased blurring of insignia and signs of today's nation state.

All these motifs were printed using a printing technique, in which inks
are mixed on a single printing cylinder. Through the rotation of the
cylinder, the colour sections change their position slightly during the
printing process. Hence, each print is unique. A standard industrial
process of reproduction is modified specifically to produce original
variety.

Poster-Edition Europe^{n}, 2012
by Oliver Klimpel

"Désirer, c'est construire un ensemble": to desire means to construct a whole, as Gilles Deleuze put it. This introduces a utopia – the idea of a something shared – into the equation. Just as this dream, the identity also wants to leave the safe haven of irony and detached relations and be a visual programme for Europe – a programme that does not shy away from the most simple and profane device an identity could make use of: a mark, a logo, a badge. The archaic simplicity of a (almost singular) logo seemed an interesting avenue to pursue.

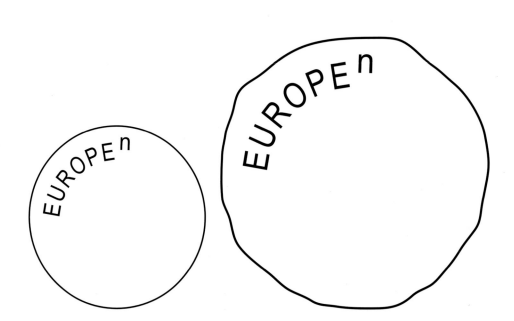

The two badge-siblings, which work individually or together

Furthermore, the general concept for the overall identity puts emphasis on an individualised, de-centralised approach in regards to the graphic styles of announcements, printed matter, and other promotional material about the projects taking place in the print workshops in Høvikodden near Oslo, Donostia – San Sebastián, or Minsk. This allowed for the expression of specific contexts through local styles and preferences of the institutions, of the curators, of the collaborators. Everything was possible – there were no no-go areas. The identity became a format of enquiry in which the question was asked: what relationship had the local project to the project *Europe (to the power of) n* as a whole? What kind of union, or communion, was discussed? Which closeness and association did the local partner feel like emphasising visually, or which style wars were fought? This approach allowed for telling comparisons between the outcomes. Since it was considered an interface, a hinge, the graphic identity touched upon a delicate issue of identification with the project. Positioning, scale, and the quantity of usage communicated a relationship with some of the premises of *Europe (to the power of) n:* exploration, trust, and exchange, which were not only on the terms of one's own choosing.

This identity used two badges that were graphic siblings and carried the name of a complicated thing: Europe. They were conceived as containers and vessels for a void or coins that were logos without a subject, in a shape that is both complicated and primitive. There were two main versions, which differ only in contour. Occupation without presence is not considered a predominant aim of building a graphic identity. Here it arguably was. Their subject was the relationship with their surrounding and between themselves. In architecture, there is a school of thought around the practice of Dutchman Rem Koolhaas who creates buildings that look like diagrams. Our logos performed the task of real-time sketches. So, besides the only occasionally reoccurring typeface which is Arial in regular and narrow, *Europe (to the power of) n's* identity was based on a different, a somewhat schizophrenic logo, that occupied spaces of various scale and significance in the eleven different cities, and was accompanied by the arbitrary local tastes and preferences.

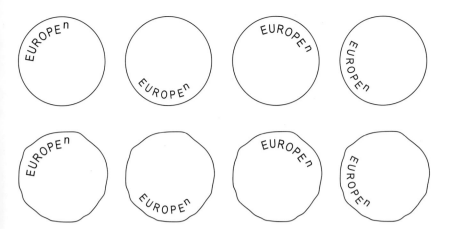

COMPETITIVE EDGES

Every company has an identity today: every art space, every initiative, every project, commercial or alternative, non-profit or not. So what could branding mean for a heavily contested and ambiguous and multifaceted entity, or political monstrosity? Since Bill Clinton's second election campaign in 1996, politics have made the transition into the management of individual desires. It abandoned the pursuit of grand ideas. Advised by the American political strategist Dick Morris, long-term values, ideologies, and utopias were replaced by responsive, short-term focus groups driven by consumerist management of crowds. Through PR, politics had adopted a model of business introducing identity and branding to this field.

Historically, visual identities in graphics have been driven either by commerce or politics, indicating possession or credit the maker. There were to mark extended family property that became kingdoms, nation states and political movements utilised coats of arms, insignia, and flags.

But since Edward Bernays, Sigmund Freud's nephew, invented public relations in the US at the beginning of the 1920s, business communications have dominated communication in capitalism, employing sophisticated analysis that tapped into people's immediate wishes. If what the political scientist Joseph Nye says is true – that the traditional hegemonic powers are now superseded by soft powers; and nation states rely on networks of influence that are persuading their numerous partners in order to swing decisions, economic contracts, and strategic alliances their way – then this also has consequences for visual relationships. If traditional graphic representations of countries through flags and traditional insignia have been eroded by the increased frequency and hybridisation of globalised trade and of their graphic symbols, then this means, paradoxically, that the dependency on visual signs and narratives has not been reduced but significantly increased. We are seeing a competition between different graphic fictions. The elusive and polemical shapes of *Europe (to the power of) n* are some of them.

SCARS AND STRIPES

In the austere, or minimal, mostly black-and-white environment of the logos and texts, "Flags" are additional, contrary objects within the discourse of *Europe (to the power of) n*'s identity. It is a series of prints produced for the worldwide branches of the Goethe-Institut to articulate an aspect of the project. The colourful vertical sections of varying width seem to form banners with lined gradients; the static yet fluent formats are reminiscent of cloth which is used to represent nation states or companies, and their increasingly blurred insignias. In the series "Flags" clearly defined colours merge and are combined with muted ones that make association more difficult. The crests and emblems have been cut and removed. These motifs were created using split fountain printing, a rare technique, in which inks are mixed next to one another on a single printing cylinder. During the printing process, the colour sections change their position slightly, through the rotation of the cylinder, and so each print becomes a one-off. A standard industrial process of reproduction is specifically modified to produce an original variety within a seemingly restricted system.

Die Frage, ob mit Europa ein Konzept gemeint ist, das sich durch ein spezifisches Territorium definiert, oder ob es dabei primär um kulturelle Verbindungen geht, wird gegenwärtig intensiv verhandelt.
Christian Teckert (Wien)

Ist es möglich, sich ein Europa vorzustellen, das bis zu einem gewissen Grade einem mittelalterlichen Szenario aus technokratischen Clans ähnelt, etwa im Jahr 2078?
Felp Agarre (San Sebastián)

Der Kontinent war niemals eine hermetisch abgeschlossene ethnische Einheit. Diese Vorstellung spiegelt lediglich die Nostalgie einer temporären Konstellation in der jüngsten Geschichte wider. Die Identität unseres (und jedes anderen) Kontinents ließe sich eher anhand eines fortschreitenden genetischen Austauschs definieren als durch eine engstirnige Fokussierung auf ethnische Standards, die sich im Verlauf der Geschichte kontinuierlich weiterentwickelt haben.
Felp Lapran (Minsk)

Angesichts globalökonomischer und geopolitischer Ereignisse, deren Zeuge man durch die unumgängliche Linse der Medien wird, ist es manchmal nicht möglich, sich des Eindrucks eines Verlusts der Verhältnismäßigkeit zu erwehren, eines tief empfundenen Gefühls, dass jegliche Möglichkeit zur Angemessenheit in unserem Verhältnis zu diesen Ereignissen und entsprechenden Entscheidungen gänzlich unausführbar ist. Zeitgenössische Konzepte von Europa haben nicht nur innerhalb ihrer jüngst hysterisch erzählten Episoden einen ähnlichen Effekt bei vielen Menschen – ein nachklingender Mangel an Proportion und in der Folge an Angemessenheit konstruktiver Handlungen in deren Konzeption, Konstruktion und Konsumption.
Silas Krieger (Leipzig / London)

Heute wird die Verantwort hinsichtlich der Folgen für ehemalige Kolonialstaaten. 2010 berichtete BBC News und Computer, die gefähr werden trotz Verbot noch exportiert. [...] Ihre Bestimm. Asien, wo sie unter widrigs zerlegt werden.
Ali Hammoudi (London)

Was ist Europa? Wo beginnt Europa, welche Länder gehören zur EU und welche nicht? Ist Europa eine geografische, historische oder kulturelle Konstruktion? Gibt es eine europäische Identität oder eine europäische Identifizierungskrise? All diese derzeitigen Probleme und Diskussionen, die in Europa stattfinden, erhalten eine andere Gewichtung und Wertigkeit, sobald man die 'Konstruktion Europa' von einem entfernten Standpunkt betrachtet.
Jan Ying (Taipei)

Konsums, des Luxus und der (vermeintlichen) Qualität den Namen „Europa", im Sinne eines Etiketts eines bestimmten europäischen Standards. Auch in Minsk, der Hauptstadt von Belarus, überragt das neu errichtete Fünf-Sterne-Hotel „Europa" das Zentrum. Abgesehen von Äußerlichkeiten sind Bekenntnisse zu Europa selten und vom aktuellen politischen Kalkül abhängig.
Lena Prents (Minsk)

Drei mögliche Szenarien über Europa: Im ersten enthält Europa wirtschaftliche und ideologische Enklaven, scheint „Europa" weder der entfernte Feind, der durch propagandistisches Fernsehen vermittelt wird. Und im letzten ist Europa ein unfruchtbares Land, das von afrikanischen Subventionen abhängt.
Ali Hammoudi (London)

Subventionen für die Landwirtschaft, die fast die Hälfte des Budgets der EU ausmachen, waren lange dafür berühmt-berüchtigt, Exzesse zu produzieren: Berge aus Butter und Seen aus Wein. Heutzutage verschieben sich die Grundlagen. Ein neues landwirtschaftliches Denkmodell, in dem Subventionen von der Produktion abgekoppelt sind, hat sich herausgebildet. Die Bauern erhalten keine Hilfsgelder mehr für die Überproduktion, sondern dafür, sich als ökologische Unternehmer und Landschaftshüter neu zu erfinden. Sie sollen nicht mehr Nahrung liefern, sondern offene Felder vorhalten.
Markus Miessen / Felix Vogel (Berlin)

Kann Europa grundsätzlich als finanzieller Raum verstanden werden? Welche Rolle nimmt dieser Raum innerhalb des globalen Finanzmarkts ein, respektive ist die Unterscheidung zwischen globalem und europäischem Finanzmarkt überhaupt möglich?
Markus Miessen / Felix Vogel (Berlin)

Mit der globalen Wirtschaftskrise am Ende der ersten und am Beginn der zweiten Dekade des 21. Jahrhunderts wird offensichtlich, dass der Status einer „Kultur im Wandel" oder einer „Gesellschaft im Wandel" nicht den postsozialistischen und postkolonialen Gesellschaften der Zweiten und Dritten Welt, welche eigentlich durch die Globalisierung in das kapitalistische Wirtschaftsmarktsystem integriert werden sollten, vorbehalten ist. Sogar die entwickelten Gesellschaften des Westens (Vereinigte Staaten, EU, Japan, Australien) befinden sich plötzlich inmitten von Prozessen, über die die Wirtschaft die Kontrolle verliert und welche die stabile Ordnung von Beherrschung, Kontrolle und Vorherrschaft des Staates zu einem unerwarteten 'Übergangsgeschehen' deterritorialisierter Netze körperschaftlichen Interesses und Kapitals transformieren. In anderen Worten, das globale System selbst ist in einen Zustand des Wandels eingetreten, der Krisensituationen und Ereignisse hervorbringt, die möglicherweise in andere, unerwartete Richtungen führen.
Miklo Savreton (Novi Sad)

Heutzutage damit beschäftigt eine pragmatische Überlebensschlacht zu führen und eine Krise zu bewältigen, scheint „Europa" weder für seine Einwohner noch für seine Nachbarn neue Gemeinschaftswerte oder -bedeutungen zu generieren. Die Revolten, die derzeit durch verschiedene Teile der Welt, unter anderem durch Europa, fegen, haben neben der Forderung nach Fortsetzung des Sozialstaates und sozialer Sicherheit auf eine radikale Neuverteilung des Wohlstands und auf Veränderungen in den Produktionsweisen und der Staatsführung gedrängt.
Justina Schröbowka vom Jarosław Lubiak (Lódź)

Es scheint, dass parallel zu den Bemühungen der Türkei, der Europäischen Union beizutreten, sich viele Menschen in der Türkei – zumindest jene, die in den Großstädten leben – die Frage gestellt haben „Bin ich Europäer?" Die Türkei ist geografisch ein großes Territorium – mit einem sich stark vom Westen unterscheidenden Osten – in dem es für jemanden, der in Istanbul lebt, wahrscheinlich naheliegender ist, sich solchen Fragen zu widmen, als für jemanden aus einer Stadt im Osten. Die Geografie, die Kultur und die Vergangenheit des Landes, dessen Arterien bis auf den Balkan und in den Mittleren Osten reichen, gaben den Menschen die Möglichkeit, über Europa als einen „anderen Ort" nachzudenken.
Esra Sarıgedik Öktem (Istanbul)

Ich würde sogar sagen, dass es in China gar keine EU oder ein Europa gibt – es gibt nur einzelne Nationen, die an die Tür eines potenziellen Wirtschaftspartners klopfen.
Jun Yang (Taipei)

Europe^n, 17.7. 2012 – 30. 4. 2013
Muzeum Sztuki, Łódź; Curating Contemporary Art Department / Royal College of Art, London; Henie Onstad Kunstsenter, Høvikodden / Oslo; Contemporary Art Study Centre / European Humanities University, Vilnius; Novaja Europa Magazine, Minsk; Galerie Y, Minsk; SALT, Istanbul; Muzej savremene umetnosti Vojvodine, Novi Sad, Sint-Lukasgalerie, Brussels; Taipei Contemporary Art Centre, Taipei; Vitamin Creative Space, Beijing / Guangzhou; Office for European Capital of Culture 2016, San Sebastián

Handelsbilanzüberschuss des Euroraums (ER 17) bei 2,8 Mrd. Euro

In der EU wohnen 51 Mio. junge Erwachsene bei ihren Eltern.

17% der EU-Bürger gelten als armutsgefährdet.

222635 Asylanträge wurden in EU27 Ländern gestellt.

Sparquote der privaten Haushalte im Euroraum auf 13,7 von 11,8 % gestiegen

99 Prozent der Luxemburger beherrschen mindestens eine Fremdsprache. Ihnen folgen die Slowaken mit 97 Prozent und die Letten mit 95 Prozent.

Höchste Anzahl an SMS Nachrichten je Einwohner in Litauen und Irland

Die Zahl der Einwohner je katholischem Priester ist in Europa um 42 gestiegen.

Flyer design for the
"Thinking Europe"-Conference

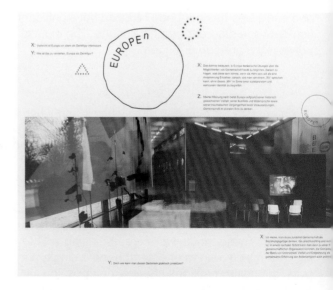

GOETHE
INSTITUT

Allianz
Kulturstiftung

Various motifs of the
poster-edition *Europe*^{n}, 2012,
different paper stocks

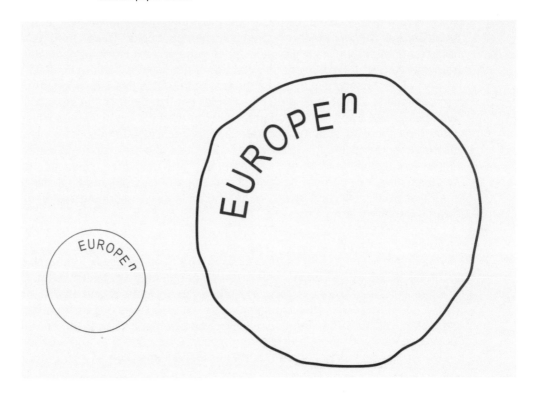

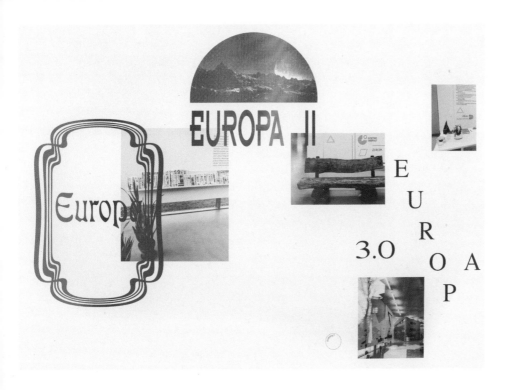

Designing the Book that Is TWO *

Oliver Klimpel

This project wants to avoid the trap of becoming a representational project, and object, about Europe. But as formats of communication go, books still can engage a public that is far greater than visiting audiences of singular exhibitions, in particular when they are cluttered over the continent. It is not books themselves that are conservative. Traditional or conservative might be the ways of reading them, or writing their texts, or constructing the thread that carries the reader through them. In the case of this book, we narrate the artistic positions through the filter of a casual magazine-like object that steers clear of the imposing stature of academia. This publishing format spans historically from obscure counter-culture to the liberating vulgarities of consumerist mainstream propaganda. Its editorial structure and heterogeneity form deliberate challenges to the recent academic turn and scholarly designs of contemporary independent publishing. A promise of popular accessibility sits side-by-side with a carefully calibrated level of obstruction towards the object of desire.

Just as *Europe (to the power of) n* appears in the form of two logos, this book is also only complete together with its predecessor: *The Scenario-Book.* Whereas the book about the foregone speculative and research period of the project is a low-key text-driven discursive affair, the second one takes you to locations and objects, to places and people and unexpected cats in galleries. It is full of pictures and environments. It rather resembles a colourful bazaar, or a full shop window that has arranged some carefully curated objects and ideas from different places, which speak to one another. The two books couldn't be more different but still share the same DNA.

* Be reminded: book lovers never go to bed alone!

Novi Sad

When the project started, one frequently asked question was: why Novi Sad and not Belgrade? Yet from the beginning, the focus was placed on the Autonomous Province Vojvodina with Novi Sad as its administrative centre. The territory of the Vojvodina underwent many changes and the various political and cultural influences have also shaped the cityscape of its capital. Smaller buildings in the city centre – which remind of the rule of the Austrian-Hungarian Empire – can be found next to Modernist, urban developments, reminiscent of the Yugoslavian era, and the remnants of rural villages next to urban developments. For *Europe (to the power of) n*, the fact that more than twenty-six ethnic groups live together in a relatively small region was decisive for Novi Sad as project venue. The largest ethnic groups are Serbs followed by Hungarians. In 2005, several international organisations, including the European Parliament and Human Rights Watch, expressed concern about rising levels of ethnic tension and related violent incidents in the Vojvodina. Today, Vojvodina is part of Serbia, which officially applied for EU membership in 2009. The multi-ethnic reality of Vojvodina is in constant conflict with nationalist groups in Serbia fighting for ethnic purity whatever the price.

http://www.novisad.rsw

ASYMMETRIC EUROPE

MUSEUM OF
CONTEMPORARY ART
VOJVODINA

COMPLEXITY
AND COMPLICITY

POLONA TRATNIK WITH COLLABORATORS
Hair in Vitro, 2011

IRWIN
Time for a New State.
Some Say You Can Find
Happiness There, 2012
(installation view)

Vreme je za ⸻vu državu.
Kažu da tamo može e naći sreću.

Miško Šuvaković

The exhibition *Asymmetric Europe* was staged at the Museum of Contemporary Art of Vojvodina in Novi Sad as part of the transcultural and transnational project *Europe (to the power of) n*. The exhibition and accompanying catalogue sought to problematise contemporary European identities, both locally (Serbia, Vojvodina, Novi Sad) and globally (Serbia, Vojvodina, Croatia, Germany, Japan, Taiwan, Austria, Turkey, the Netherlands, Belarus, Sweden, Poland, England, France, USA).

When the project was realised in Germany, England, Belarus, Poland, Turkey, Norway, Serbia/Vojvodina, Belgium, Spain/Basque Country, and China, it acquired different forms of artistic and cultural interactions with those countries's local contexts. The exhibition *Asymmetric Europe* took place in Novi Sad between 16 November and 2 December 2012, precisely when Serbia's political and social antagonisms surrounding the status of the autonomous province of Vojvodina and the question of accepting or rejecting the European Union, were coming to a head. The exhibition appeared in the context of a museum at a time when the debate about Serbia's European identity and affiliation was unfolding as the central problem of Serbia's society. The exhibition drew the attention of Serbia and Vojvodina's mass media (newspapers, political magazines, television programmes) and showed that the issue of Europe and what is European is a central issue of Serbia/Vojvodina's contemporary politics, culture, and art.

The exhibition was set up on the conceptual model of debating complexity and complicity in relation to the positions of European contemporary artists.

On the Edge of Europe

Novi Sad, capital of Vojvodina, is today one of the cultural centres of Serbia (besides Belgrade) with around thirty nationalities and languages. Belgrade and Novi Sad are located on the same European river, the Danube, but culturally they belong to different realms of history, language, and rule: on the one hand there is the heritage of the Austrian-Hungarian Empire, on the other there is the centuries-long border with the Byzantium and the Ottoman Empire.

The exhibition in Novi Sad is the only part of *Europe (to the power of) n* to take place in Serbia, the Western Balkans. This perspective is, therefore, essential; from the far edge to the so-called centre of Europe. Here, a lot of attention is given to Europe and to the exhibition curated by Miško Šuvaković. According to polls, a deep scepticism prevails in Serbia about Europe, even among the younger generation. The country is divided into advocates for and opponents

against Europe. There are strong sympathies for Russia, who stood by Serbia in hard times, in opposition to Europe and its political powers. There are antipathies against NATO, the EU, and Germany on account of the Nazi occupation in the 1940s and the NATO bombing of Belgrade and of Novi Sad in 1999. But there is a desire to look forward: 2012 was an election year, a year of change. The political sphere is doing everything to ensure that the EU membership talks can take place as soon as possible. Is this only rhetoric, or will this lead to concrete governmental action? Is it simply a matter of time before the border issues with Kosovo are resolved through sustained dialogue and pragmatic solutions, or will they remain irresolvable and suppressed: a potentially explosive marginalia on the edge of the long ago pacified Western Balkans.

A senior Belgian politician is quoted to have said in the recent press, "It is absurd that 100 years after the Balkan wars the Western Balkans is still not a part of Europe". "Who cares what

129

happens in the small province of Vojvodina, which is neither large nor powerful nor even a bit heroic?" the curator asked on the occasion of the exhibition with a twinkle in his eye. Concluding, I would say: in the multi-ethnic territory of Vojvodina, a historically transitory space of Europe, on the edge of the strong central Europe and of important national centres *Europe (to the power of) n* has found a resonant expression.

Europe's complexity has been presented by means of models of complicit dialogues regarding artists who have "tested" their practice in relation to the public and private narratives of Europe (politics, the everyday, intimacy, science, individuality, collectivity, freedom, rigidity, mobility, otherness, community). Therefore, the exhibition's theoretical conception may be posited quite explicitly in a single sentence: the central problem of life and art today is how to articulate the visibility of a plurality that eludes a consistent expression of a nation, state, class, gender, generation, and global geographic identity.
Asymmetric Europe was structured by several parallel regimes[1] of performing Europe's hybrid and asymmetric, individual and collective *body*. The exhibition at the Museum of Contemporary Art of Vojvodina featured post-media artworks (photographs, video works, paintings, diagrams, objects, architectural models) made in the context of South-East Europe. The exhibition presented works by the IRWIN group, Tadej Pogačar, and Polona Tratnik (Slovenia), Nika Radić (Croatia/Germany), Zoran Todorović, Dejan Grba, Jovan Čekić, Nataša Teofilović (Serbia), Zorica Čolić, Živko Grozdanić, Dragomir Ugren (Vojvodina). The artistic platform *Provisional SALTA Ensemble* was taken up from the transcultural context of an exchange between Beirut, Berlin, and Belgrade.

A film programme was realised, which served to index a "symptom" of contemporary culture in a permanent state of emergency featuring work by Nika Radić (Zagreb, Berlin), Jun Yang (Taipei, Vienna, Yokohama), Köken Ergun (İstanbul, Berlin), Aleksander Komarov (Amsterdam, Minsk), IRWIN (Ljubljana), Annika Eriksson (Stockholm, Berlin), the ABS group (Krk, Rijeka, Dubrovnik), Boris Bezić & Janez Janša, Janez Janša, Janez Janša (Ljubljana). This selection of artists and their films produced a direct link with the curatorial choices presented in *Scenarios about Europe*, a series of presentations displayed at the Museum of Contemporary Art, Leipzig. As both the curator and artist, Jun Yang showed one of his own films. Turkish curator Esra Sarigedik Öktem

---

1   The term "regime" is pragmatically used here in reference to Jacques Rancière's concept of "regimes of art", a mode of articulation between three things: ways of doing and making, their corresponding forms of visibility, and ways of conceptualising both the former and the latter.

NIKA RADIĆ
The End, 2012

TADEJ POGAČAR
P.A.R.A.S.I.T.E. Public Sculpture,
1999–2010

selected the film and video artist Köken Ergun. The Belarusian / German curator Lena Prents decided on the artist Aleksander Komarov and Spanish / Basque curator Peio Aguirre chose the artist Annika Eriksson. The point was to stage a dialogic exchange between different film works and various curatorial choices in the context of the exhibition in Novi Sad. The project also comprised lecture performances by Slavs and Tatars and IRWIN. Polish curators Joanna Sokołowska and Jarosław Lubiak selected Slavs and Tatars for their third scenario exhibition in Leipzig, however, in the Novi Sad exhibition a discursive relation between Slavs and Tatars's lecture performance *Chains We Can Believe In* and *NSK State in Time* by IRWIN's Miran Mohar was drawn upon. In their work, Slavs and Tatars establish a critical and ecstatic relationship between Islamic and Western narratives of identifying and self-identifying in a global world. The IRWIN group made a dialectical turn from reconstructing Eastern Europe's post-socialist identity toward producing the global identity of a state in time.

A debate titled *Curating Europe* took place between curators (Barbara Steiner, Joanna Sokołowska, Kit Hammonds, and Miško Šuvaković) and artists (Nika Radić and Miran Mohar) who engaged in a dialogue on the relationship between curatorial and artistic labour in contemporary conditions of Europe. The dialogue and complicity in this debate offered a theorisation of the international political context in relation to the exhibition *Asymmetric Europe* within the specific context of Serbia and Vojvodina.

Artists:
Jovan Čekić, Zorica Čolić, Dejan Grba, Živko Grozdanić, IRWIN, Tadej Pogačar, Provisional SALTA Ensemble, Nika Radić, Zoran Todorović, Nataša Teofilović, Polona Tratnik, Dragomir Ugren, Boris Bezić, Köken Ergun, Annika Eriksson, Group ABS, Aleksander Komarov, Nika Radić, Slavs and Tatars, Jun Yang

DRAGOMIR UGREN
Untitled (wall installation), 2011

PROVISIONAL SALTA ENSEMBLE
Monument (Desire for Democracy), 2012

PROVISIONAL SALTA ENSEMBLE
Monument (Desire for Democracy), 2012

ASIMETRIČNA EVROPA:
POTENCIJALNOST, SLOŽENOST I
SAUČESNIŠTVO

metric

rope

Asimetričn

Evropa

Scenarios about Europe

Asymmetric Europe, 2012
Catalogue design by Oliver Klimpel,
with Dragomir Ugren

ZORAN TODOROVIĆ
The Bride, 1998

ZORICA ČOLIĆ
Face Shifting, 2005–2007

134

The reasons for choosing Brussels for *Europe (to the power of) n* – a project that seeks to challenge ideas of a powerful exclusive European community from peripheral positions – seems to be misleading at first sight. Clearly, Brussels is a centre: it is the capital of Belgium, an important centre for international and for the European Union's politics. In the project, however, "peripheral" refers to the fragile relationship of the cities (and countries) chosen with a self-identifying "core" Europe. Alongside this, doubts about its substantial and exclusive identity arise. Brussels was considered to be a significant case in this regard: being a "fragile" capital and a "fragile" centre of the European Union. It is a highly diverse, multi-ethnic and global city; it is a city in which tensions between Walloons and the Flemings can be mapped, as in the entire Belgium. The final decision for Brussels was made in 2010. At that time, there was a headline in the *Süddeutsche Zeitung:* "Adieu Belgium, adieu Europe! Nationalism is on the rise, for Europe this does not mean anything good". The text polemically recommended the EU to leave Brussels due to europhobic tendencies in Belgium.

---

http://www.brussels.be

EUROPEAN ECONOMIC AND SOCIAL
COMMITTEE

AND

COMMITTEE OF THE REGIONS

CULTURAL FREEDOM IN EUROPE

GOETHE-INSTITUT BRÜSSEL

ENRIQUE MARTY
Fall of the Idols, 2013
(installation view)

REZA ARAMESH
Action 108, 2007–2013

CLEGG & GUTTMANN
Board of Directors, 2007

DAVIDE BERTOCCHI
Le Régime, 2009

HEIDI VOET
Stars & Constellations, 2012
(coins on floor)

TONY MATELLI
Yesterday, 2009

TIM EITEL
Architect, 2012

HELMUT STALLAERTS
Die Auflösung, 2009

Display Elements designed by Christian Teckert and Christine Bock with poster-edition by Oliver Klimpel

Significant for Europe is the continuous questioning of its identity. What could be the common denominator to unite more than half a billion people? It seems that geography, history, religion, or descent are unable to provide a balanced answer, and it is questionable whether a hybrid culture can offer a solution. The only remaining inclusive element that could bring together all Europeans on an equal basis is their creative potential. Throughout European history there has been an undercurrent of self-critical reflection, in which the people have dared to doubt the foundations of the existing society. This exhibition takes its unique position from the fact that it questions Europe from within the European district in Brussels, more particularly being hosted at the European Economic and Social Committee, the Committee of the Regions and the Goethe-Institut Brussels.

One assumption of the exhibition is that the creative potential of life starts with genetic freedom. Central to Koen Vanmechelen's *Cosmopolitan Chicken Project* is the crossbreeding of chickens. The artist interbreeds domestic chickens from different countries aiming at the creation of the true cosmopolitan chicken as a symbol for global diversity. From an early age, humans are fundamentally exposed to external influences. Education is one of the main influences in our lives, and it is a field, in which the social impact on the individual is particularly strong. Ane Hjort Guttu's film *Freedom Requires Free People* shows the conflict between human nature and a kind of learned or trained behaviour. Enrique Marty's installation *The Fall of the Idols* goes back to the roots of civilisation and encourages an imaginary dimension of the past. The artist has produced sculptures based on popular interpretations of gods. What belongs to the core of a society at a certain time can be a source of misinterpretation and new meanings for later generations. What often remains is how we are impressed by iconic images. Philip Metten creates his own hybrid system that disturbs stereotyped interpretations and invites us to participate in the production of symbolic meaning. Josephine Meckseper displays fetish-like objects in vitrines. The objects are meant to seduce the viewer on an aesthetic, erotic, and consumerist level. However, this strategy is subverted by the artist and transformed by a political analysis of how our economic system is based on image building, false expectations, and inequality. As Helmut Stallaerts's office photos demonstrate, we are all heavily indebted to the learned patterns of collective behaviour. This is also shown in Clegg and Guttmann's portraits of the powerful. They look staged and as if they are playing roles. This is in contrast to the homeless people depicted in the paintings of Tim Eitel or as photographed by Reza Aramesh. The latter reconstructs poignant scenes of contemporary history as we know them through mass media, but contextualises them in sumptuous environments of European history. Tim Eitel's painting *The Architect* shows a meditative intellectual in a Roma refugee camp. There is an aesthetic force in the representation of the slums, which is also visible in Hannes Schmid's photos *New Dump 1 to 6* that show the living conditions of Asian street children as a by-product of the global economy. Meanwhile, Europe and Asia have become strongly intertwined on a level of investment and consumption. The official Europe stands miles away from the shady sides of politics. Nedko Solakov operates as an acute commentator of political events, taking into consideration human failure. Visual stories are close to fairy tales originating from an undefined notion of time and space. They work like little comments made at the margins of official ceremonies. The film *Anygirl* by goldiechiari speaks of the wave of political / criminal homicides that scourged Italy (and other countries) between the 1950s and the 1980s. Davide Bertocchi's sculpture *Le Régime* refers to the budget cuts after years of misgovernment and pressure on the justice system in Italy. In Rainer Ganahl's film *Der Schweinehirt (Swineherd)* pigs are fed by their shepherd with (faked) 100-Euro notes. The basic economy of farming and the picturesque setting stay in sharp contrast to the abstract banking system.

Many aspects of contemporary life have become so complicated that they can only be understood on an abstract level. The conceptual paintings by Eberhard Havekost and Frank Nitsche offer a synthesis of our fragmented visual experience. One could almost assume that our vision of Europe is indebted to the way our brain deals with the mathematical structures defining the world. What remains are vague fragments of endlessly transformed images. Heidi Voet's installation *Stars & Constellations* displays coins from different continents and political systems. Among them, there is one newly produced coin resembling the Euro, which the artist gained permission to produce from the European Central Bank. The eleven stars of the Euro look like Chinese stars and the centre of this coin lacks any national symbol. Additionally, the work reminds of a firmament, it refers to charity and even to the irrational moment of throwing coins into fountains. Ariel Schlesinger presents a photo of a view through a window. Looking closer one sees that the artwork displays cracks on various levels. The fissures in the photographed window are carefully doubled in the glass frame. Premeditated "destruction" turns into a poetic dimension. In the exhibition, the critical evaluation of Europe is in the unfolding potentialities for a renewed continent.

Cultural Freedom in Europe

PHILIP METTEN
Untitled, 2011

SYLVIE FLEURY
A Journey to Fitness or How to
Loose 10 Pounds in 3 Weeks,
1993–1998
(installation view)

VERONICA BROVALL
Coexist, 2011

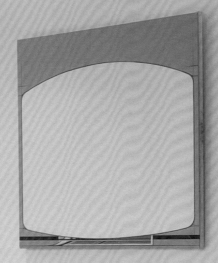

FRANK NITSCHE
EYE-16-2013, 2013; SEM-17-2013, 2013;
WCH-18-2013, 2013; GIL-19-2013, 2013
(installation view)

Europe (to the power of) n in Brussels

"Freedom", perhaps the greatest European word, can be best expressed in French. The German word (see Kant or Hölderlin) is *Frieden* (peace). It is evident that *Liberté* is the ideal concept Europe could sail upon today, whereas the narrative of peace as a post-war European motif has lost its effectiveness, despite the warnings and admonitions of our elders.

Freedom, liberté? If only it were that simple! In a permissive society, the awareness of the worth of freedom seems to fade away, just as it was the case after the end of the war, almost seventy years ago, with peace. Its meaning returns, as in Belarus or in the Balkans, when it is in danger.

This is why we need art, at best at the centre of European affairs: in the hallways of the European Economic and Social Committee and the Committee of the Regions; in the anonymous glass boxes of uptown Brussels, and in the airless, lousy buildings of central Europe that take one's breath away and in which thousands of European officials, politicians, media people and lobbyists try to develop something like a "European enthusiasm".

In addition, experts talk about "The Cultural Freedom in Europe". With a title like this, scepticism is indicated. "Culture", "freedom", "Europe" – three vast terms that could keep hundreds of Europhilic Sunday conversationalists very busy. What does it mean?

Does art need freedom? (Yes) Does it need freedom of speech and freedom of expression? (Obviously) An absence of censorship? (This goes without saying) Are artists free people? (Contrary to common preconceptions, they are often rather more driven) Do all people and all minorities need cultural freedom? (Yes, of course, but what does that mean?) As always, we end up with more questions than answers.

Freedom and criticism are conjoined twins, they are "fundamental concepts of Europe" as mentioned by the Brussels curator Filip Luyckx in his opening speech. Precisely because art is the channel, which spreads the immense European potential of criticism and self-criticism, it has been the basis of our European culture throughout Greek antiquity, the Christian tradition, and the Enlightenment.

And now art should prove itself in the corridors of the European administration. The artworks Luyckx has gathered will not have a hard time in a setting that is usually attuned to a pragmatic daily schedule. But passersby get the opportunity to come into contact with art where it is not normally seen, and to confront issues that go beyond the pragmatism of the everyday.

KOEN VANMECHELEN
Pedigree – CCP, 2013
(installation view)

Artists:
Michaël Aerts, Reza Aramesh, Davide Bertocchi,
Olaf Breuning, Veronica Brovall, Tim Eitel, Sylvie Fleury,
Clegg & Guttmann, Rainer Ganahl, Johan Van Geluwe,
goldiechiari, Ane Hjort Guttu, Eberhard Havekost,
Enrique Marty, Tony Matelli, Josephine Meckseper,
Philip Metten, Jonathan Monk, Frank Nitsche,
Nils Norman, Reynold Reynolds & Patrick Jolley,
Ariel Schlesinger, Hannes Schmid, Anne-Marie Schneider,
Nedko Solakov, Helmut Stallaerts, Koen Vanmechelen,
Heidi Voet

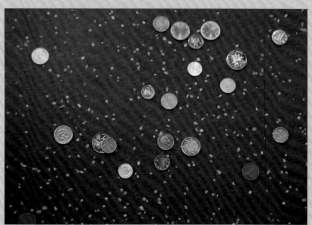

HEIDI VOET
Stars & Constellations, 2012

NEDKO SOLAKOV
Political Stories, no. 1, 2012

ARIEL SCHLESINGER
The Kid 2012, 2012

MICHAËL AERTS
Misala, 2009
(installation view)

147

ENRIQUE MARTY
Fall of the Idols, 2013
(installation view)

Advertising Europe Through Film

Florian Wüst

The idea of a united Europe has never been so tangible, so real as today with the twenty-seven member states of the European Union linked through various supranational institutions and a shared market. Beyond the free movement of goods and people, multilayered social and cultural relations create a certain sense of community. However, since the rejection of the Constitutional Treaty in public referendums in France and the Netherlands in 2005, and aggravated by the current debt crisis of the eurozone, it seems less and less clear how the political system and constitutional basis of the union will further develop. Critical attitudes towards the European Union and agitation keep rising – even in Germany.

In reaction to the actual negative image of the EU, "The committed Europeans", a group of eleven German corporate foundations, started a non-governmental initiative entitled *I want Europe* in August 2012.[1] Under the patronage of Federal President Joachim Gauck, the initiative intends to draw attention to the advantages and benefits of "Europe".[2] In order to send out "a visible and positive signal for a strong Europe", personal declarations of two dozen prominent "ambassadors" – among them former German chancellor Helmut Schmidt, football player Philipp Lahm, Daimler CEO Dieter Zetsche, and actress Bettina Zimmermann, were published on the Internet as well as in print advertisements and TV commercials. This was made possible by the support of major publishing houses and media companies like RTL Group, Axel Springer, Süddeutscher Verlag, Gruner & Jahr, and Google. Besides the celebrities, a small number of normal citizens appear in the adverts – after all, *I want Europe* claims to give "ordinary people the chance to have their say. By committing themselves to Europe and thinking about Europe, they provide food for thought and open up the European debate." Campaigns like *I want Europe* or the European Commission's video series promoting EU enlargement[3] show that the idea of a united Europe doesn't just sell by itself. It actually never did. In the early 1950s, at the very beginning of the (West) European integration process, great efforts were made to propagate the "European project" as a means to economically reconstruct and modernise the war-devastated continent. Against the background of the deepening division of the world after 1945, this process was largely supported, if not controlled by the United States. "The European integration was as much an instrument as it was a product of American hegemony in the Western world."[4] In this regard, the European Recovery Program (ERP) – first proposed in a speech by Secretary of State George Marshall at Harvard University in June 1947 – was an undoubtedly successful way to establish an anti-communist bloc, a healthy European sales market as well as a dollar-dominated system of international trade. Operational from 1948 to 1952, the so-called Marshall Plan provided sixteen European countries with financial and material aid. These were the

1 See http://www.ich-will-europa.de/

2 As in common practice, the campaign equates the term "Europe" with the European Union, or even with the much smaller eurozone, although some European countries obviously don't partake in either of them. It was never exhaustively defined, and what Europe is, where it begins and ends, culturally as well as geographically, still remains subject to change.

3 See http://ec.europa.eu/enlargement

4 Eckart Conze, "Zauberwort Europa. Die europäische Integration in Politik und Gesellschaft der Bundesrepublik Deutschland 1949–1999," in Bilanz: 50 Jahre Bundesrepublik Deutschland, eds. Marie-Luise Recker, Burkhard Jellonnek, Bernd Rauls, St. Ingbert 2001, 154 (Translation by the author).

countries that stood outside Soviet influence, except Spain. The implementation of the thirteen-billion-dollar reconstruction plan was accompanied by an extensive image and information campaign, with film playing a leading role: screened in cinemas before movies, and as part of educational programmes, the short film format promised to reach vast audiences.

The films were usually made by European film teams and production companies under the commission of the local offices of the Economic Corporation Administration (ECA) and the US government agency that managed the Marshall Plan until 1951. Many of them use a mix of documentary and fictional narrative, combined with animated sequences and charts. Stuart Schulberg's *Me and Mr. Marshall* (1949), for instance, features a young coal miner in the Ruhr area who introduces himself as "Hans Fischer, age: 26, profession: optimist". He describes the dreadful living conditions in post-war Europe and how American aid helps to increase productivity and export as the first steps to a better economic and social future. The somewhat low-brow account of the protagonist supports easy identification with the story of personal commitment necessary to meet the difficulties of the reconstruction process in a historical moment, where it was anything but granted that the majority of West Germans would follow the concept of capitalist society and the "American Way of Life". Because of their initial political indetermination and critical distance to the "occupiers", not least under the enduring influence of Nazi anti-capitalist propaganda, the United States introduced, concurrent with the Marshall Plan, a distinctly benevolent re-education policy that aimed at winning over the hearts and minds of the West Germans: by teaching them to regain self-esteem and self-initiative; to tolerate other opinions and foreign views; to trust in democracy and the rule of law; and to embrace industrial rationalisation and the idea of the free market. Here, too, film represented the medium that seemed most suitable for the communication of complex issues, and for putting them in hard contrast to the totalitarian system of former Nazi Germany or the socialist model of planned economy and centralised governance. More than fifty re-education films, produced exclusively for West German audiences between 1949 and 1952, match with the Marshall Plan films especially in those parts that concern international trade, exchange, friendship, travel and youth programmes. In short: the advocation of European integration as part of the "free" Western world.

In all these films, the image of a continent cut up by frontiers and toll bars, national egoism and enmity serves as a metaphor for the old Europe, incapable of providing prosperity and peace, security and welfare. "Let the barriers vanish. For all that we possess of energy and skill, it only yields its full reward if we are united in aim, in mind, in heart, in action. Let those who follow say of us: that in the hour of choice we chose the cause of duty to each other. That through the unity of Europe we brought the round world clos er to the unity of all mankind." With these words and rhetoric ends *The Hour of Choice*, 1951, directed by British documentarist Stuart Legg. The film deploys the thesis that Western Europe's fortune lies with international cooperation, not aiming at "anything less than a union as a whole", according to a fragment of a speech by Winston Churchill whose statement sounds like it was from a utopian past when looking at the long history of EU scepticism in the UK. One of the institutional examples presented in *The Hour of Choice* is the European Coal and Steel Community (ECSC), founded in 1951 by France, Italy, West Germany, and the Benelux states, on the initiative of French foreign minister Robert Schuman. As Europe's first supranational community, the ECSC set the ground for the future European Union by establishing a common market for coal and steel. These raw materials were substantial for post-war modern life. Over images of factory workers assembling cars, telephones, and light bulbs, Eva Kroll's *Europa im Werden – Der Schuman Plan* (1952), a newsreel-style documentary about the birth of the ECSC points out: "Coal and steel are the base of our entire civilisation. That's why the European Coal and Steel Community has to be a creation of all for all. Who has coal and steel, has it all." Advertising Western European integration the films not only celebrate what has been accomplished, but also show what more is needed in order to do away with the many man-made boundaries. *The Changing Face of Europe*, a series of six ECA films, produced in Technicolor by Wessex Film Productions, London, and distributed in thirteen different languages, assesses the achievements of the Marshall Plan some five years after the end of the war.[1] For instance, *Power for All* (1951) advocates the necessity of a Europe-wide electrical power grid. *Somewhere To Live* (1950) looks at the problem of adequate new housing, taking the war-shattered French town of Caen as an example; while *Clearing the Lines* (1951) surveys the state of transport and the dissatisfying progress made in rebuilding roads, railways, and airports. *Men and Machines* (1951) conveys the message that industrial automation and mass production must not eliminate traditional craftsmanship and the manufacture of quality goods. Aside from the tone of Cold War propaganda, some of these films stand out in their openness towards the hardships of the overwhelming processes of modernisation and globalisation. Nevertheless, and besides the fact that Europe is also described as representing a community of values, of peace and defence, democracy and human rights, none of the early campaigns for reconstructing and integrating Western Europe after 1945 disguise the leading significance of economic rationales.[2]

5   See http://www.dhm.de/filmarchiv/die-filme/changing-face-of-europe

6   Cf. Gabriele Clemens, 'Europa – nur ein gemeinsamer Markt? Die Öffentlichkeitsarbeit für den europäischen Integrationsprozess am Beispiel der Europafilme zwischen Marshallplan und Römischen Verträgen 1947–1957', in Vom gemeinsamen Markt zur europäischen Unionsbildung. 50 Jahre Römische Verträge 1957–2007, eds. Michael Gehler, Vienna/Cologne/Weimar 2009, 45–61.

EVA KROLL, Europa im Werden – Der Schuman-Plan, 1952 (film still)

Today, the association of a united Europe with corporate wealth and alleged prosperity for all obviously doesn't provide sufficient identification with what many think of when talking about the EU: excessive bureaucracy, statism, and unseizable decision making. Looking at the big business names behind *I want Europe*[7], it seems disputable whether the initiative's emphasis on a multiplicity of reasons for a joint overcoming of the current crisis "from the advantages of the economic and monetary union, peace-keeping, promotion of culture and education, climate and consumer protection to the strengthening of human and workers' rights" is credible enough to make a difference.

7   See http://www.ich-will-europa.de/en/initiative/committed-europeans

STUART LEGG,
The Hour of Choice, 1951
(film still)

EVA KROLL
Europa im Werden – Der Schuman-Plan 1952
(film still)

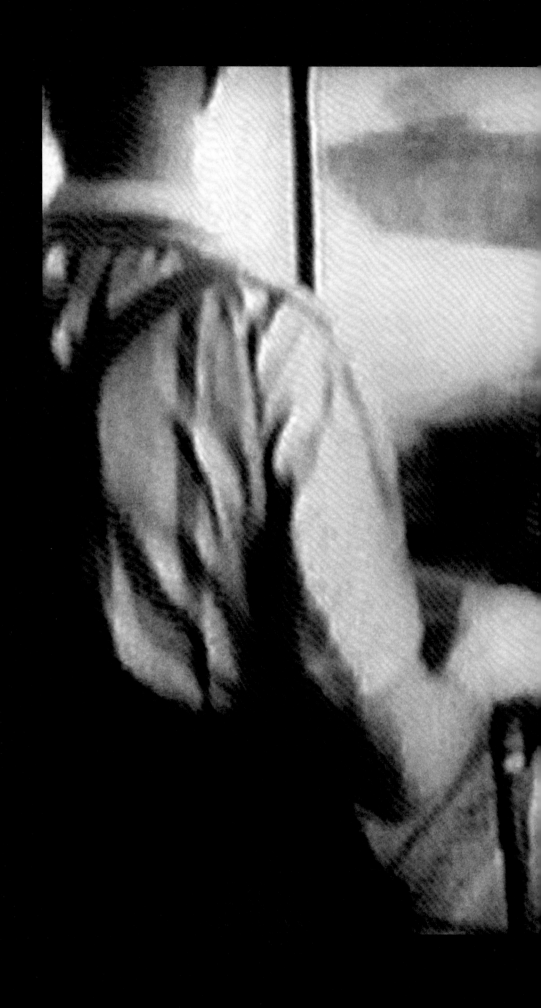

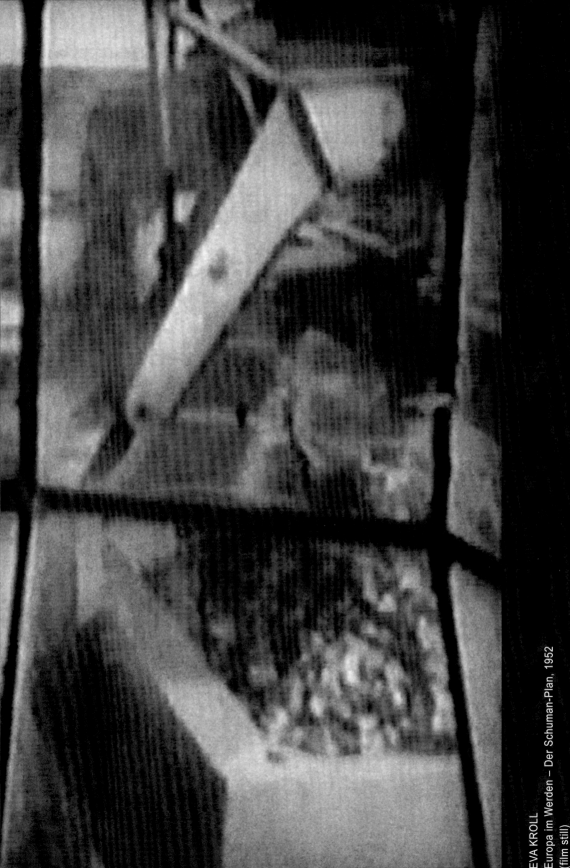

EVA KROLL
Europa im Werden – Der Schuman-Plan, 1952
(film still)

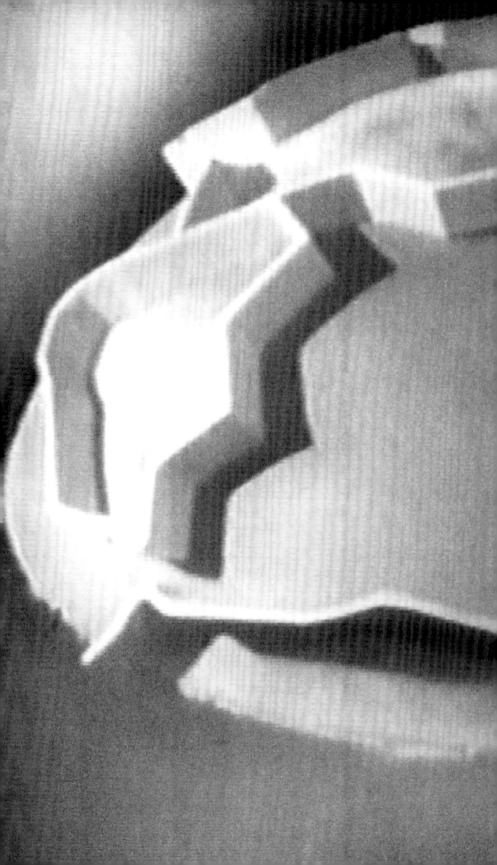

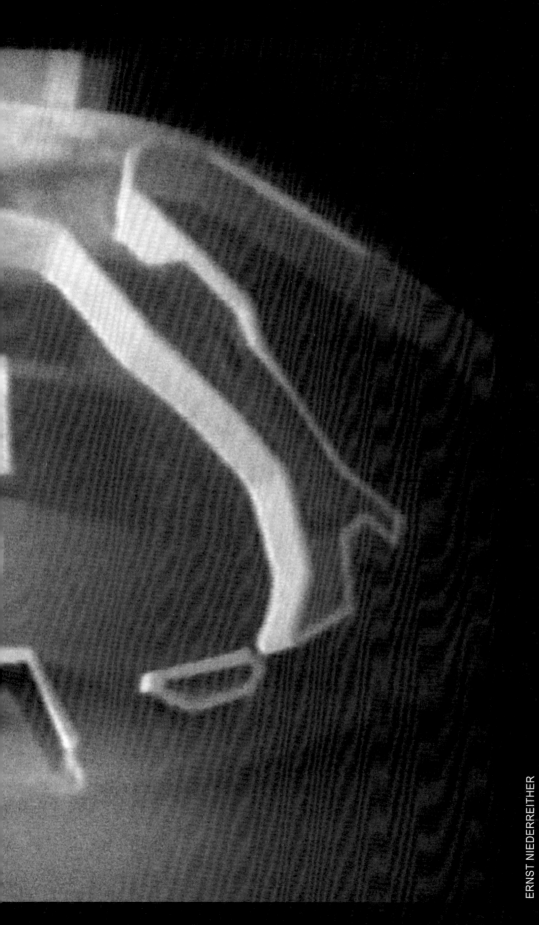

ERNST NIEDERREITHER
Wir und die Anderen, 1950
(film still)

MAN

CAHIER

LA VUE

E NOIR

L'INTERIEUR
DE LA VUE LA CLE

A EUROPEAN EXHIBITION SPACE

The architectural contribution for *Europe (to the power of) n* tries to reflect a certain desire for coherence, while at the same time speaking about the incongruencies, asymmetries, and ruptures in this attempt. It is about using basic and minimal devices in order to create a blueprint of a "European Exhibition Space". The concept consists of a set of devices for representing the heteronomy of positions embedded in the structure of this project. We tried to put into question the idea of a unified exhibition design for the series of exhibitions within *Europe (to the power of) n,* while at the same time utilising the desire for coherent representations. Therefore, we defined a set of rules, which are derived from normative, economic, and aesthetic systems that attempt to represent more or less directly certain ideas about Europe.
We suggested three basic elements to the curators to choose from in order to work with them in developing their exhibition settings. The curators could choose one aspect or a combination of those elements depending on their interest and needs.

A LINE / A SURFACE / AN OBJECT

A line drawn at exactly one metre above floor level, refers to the "Meterriss" or "Benchmark line".

This is a common technique used in a building process in order to calibrate the measurements on a building site by creating an artificial horizon. This line should be drawn directly on one or two cornered exhibition walls with an HB pencil (Hard Black) – a European standard unit – and should provide a minimal background for a part of the exhibition setting.

A surface created by using one colour referencing the series *Guggenheim Colors by Fine Paints of Europe.*

The *Gallery Colour Series* consists of a selection of wall colours favourably used by exhibition designers, artists, and curators according to an analysis of the Guggenheim Archives. These colours mostly come in shades of light grey, beige, or different whites. The difference from the chosen colour to the already existing wall colour might be minimal. The chosen colour should be applied to at least one part of the individual exhibition space above the one-metre benchmark line. Thereby, a horizon line is created that crosses and connects all exhibitions, while the chosen colours of the background speak of the subtle differences embedded within the specific spatial conceptions or preferences. In each case, this would create a minimal, sometimes hardly visible back-

ground for the exhibitions/projects. The placement of the benchmark line and the positioning of the colour field would be up to the interpretation of the individual curators (or artists) involved. Photos of the specific exhibitions were suggested to be taken from the height of one metre above ground. This common horizon created by the benchmark line plus the coloured surfaces above this line was intended to serve as the connecting element in a collage of highly heterogeneous exhibition situations. Furthermore, an imaginary exhibition space would be created, that would be a blueprint of the very incoherent and contradictory spatiality of a European Exhibition Space.

A three-dimensional object used as a tool for spatial negotiation.

The standardised size of the Euro-pallet, invented in the 1950s, represents a tool that not only makes transport more efficient, but also delineates a certain territory, as the Euro-pallet is incompatible with the global ISO container sizes and can therefore only operate effectively within European countries.
On the basis of this system, a spatial element was defined, which consists of five boxes measuring 24 × 80 × 220 cm: the maximum volume that can be put on a Euro-pallet. The individual boxes consist of shelves of differing heights, according to the European DIN paper formats. However, aside from holding books, these boxes could be used as display walls, tables, platforms, space dividers, etc. These elements served as optional devices for structuring the spaces where concrete architectural decisions were needed or wished for. They also represent an interface for possible interactions between individual curatorial concepts and the architectural dimension of *Europe (to the power of) n.* They might appear in the specific exhibitions in very different forms and might be altered substantially in their journey from one exhibition site to another.

AN (IMPOSSIBLE) EUROPEAN EXHIBITION SPACE

The architectural contribution to this project consists primarily in the design of a device, which serves as a tool for giving specific interests a visibility, but also to offer a platform for potential cross-communications and negotiations. Thereby, we also tried to create a portrait of the structure of the project as a whole, showing some common ground, but also partial interests, fragmentary aspects, and producing an unstable order of a space of possibilities: possibly the impossible "European Exhibition Space".

1   LINE (mandatory)

A line drawn directly on the chosen wall with a pencil of HB (hard black) at exactly one metre above ground floor level. (benchmark line)

At least one exhibition wall, which is representative of the whole exhibition situation, should be chosen by the curator.

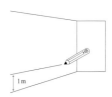

2   SURFACE (mandatory)

A surface created by using one colour based on the series *Guggenheim Colors by Fine Paints of Europe*. The chosen colour can be applied to at least a part of the individual exhibition spaces above the one-metre benchmark line.

     SENDING THE COLOUR

The Guggenheim Color Classic and Gallery Color fan deck are sent to each exhibition. The curator can choose one or two colours to apply to the chosen wall and the optional three-dimensional objects.

3   THREE-DIMENSIONAL OBJECT (optional)

Additionaly three-dimensional objects can be applied, which are based on the Euro-pallet. The objects can be used as display walls, tables, platforms, space dividers, etc. The elements can be arranged in collaboration between architects, artists, and curators to form a specified spatial setting. (see manual for customising the shelves)

     TRANSPORT / BUILDING

The curator can order any non-occupied elements for his exhibition or build their own elements. (see manual building the shelves)

The elements could be easily transported to the exhibition sites and customised in collaboration with the curators to adapt them to the specific needs and interests.

4   EXHIBITION PHOTO

A photo of the benchmark line, the chosen colour on the wall, and/or the three dimensional objects, to be taken from the height of exactly one metre above ground and parallel to the wall is asked for.

5   EUROPEAN EXHIBITION SPACE COLLAGE

Subsequently, the photo of each exhibition situation will be merged together. The common horizon created by the benchmark line plus the coloured surfaces above this line will serve as the connecting element in a collage of highly heterogeneous exhibition situations. (see next pages)

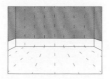

Cutting List:
5 Shelves

240 × Screws
  5 × Board A
10 × Board B
40 × Board C

199 × 70 × 0,18 cm — Board A

199 × 20,2 × 0,18 cm — Board B

1 Shelf
48 Screws

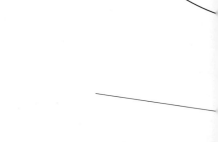

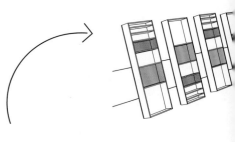

Colour

Colours can be chosen from the *Guggenheim Colors* and applied / over-painted, but the cut-edge of the plywood should be left colourless.

Colours from the previous colour layers chosen by the curators can be left visible.

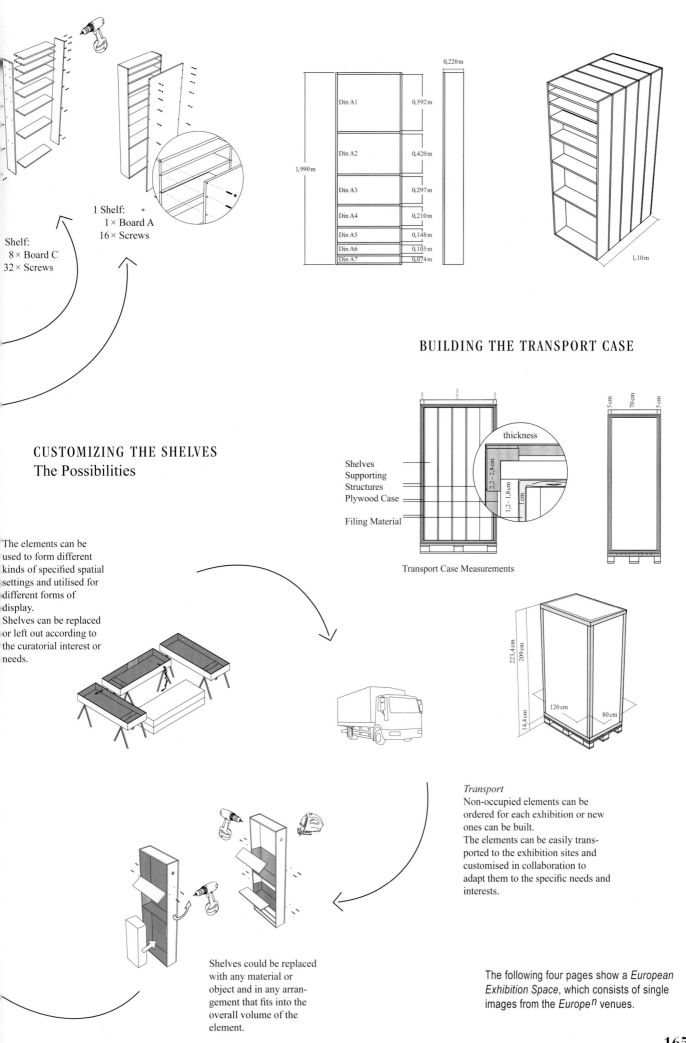

1 Shelf:
1 × Board A
16 × Screws

Shelf:
8 × Board C
32 × Screws

Din A1	0,592 m
Din A2	0,420 m
Din A3	0,297 m
Din A4	0,210 m
Din A5	0,148 m
Din A6	0,105 m
Din A7	0,074 m

1,990 m

0,220 m

1,10 m

BUILDING THE TRANSPORT CASE

thickness

Shelves
Supporting
Structures
Plywood Case

Filing Material

2,2 — 2,8 cm

1,2 — 1,8 cm

1 cm

5 cm   70 cm   5 cm

Transport Case Measurements

CUSTOMIZING THE SHELVES
The Possibilities

The elements can be used to form different kinds of specified spatial settings and utilised for different forms of display.
Shelves can be replaced or left out according to the curatorial interest or needs.

223,4 cm   209 cm

14,4 cm

120 cm   80 cm

Shelves could be replaced with any material or object and in any arrangement that fits into the overall volume of the element.

Transport
Non-occupied elements can be ordered for each exhibition or new ones can be built.
The elements can be easily transported to the exhibition sites and customised in collaboration to adapt them to the specific needs and interests.

The following four pages show a *European Exhibition Space*, which consists of single images from the *Europe[n]* venues.

_ Spatial Identity Europe (to the power of)

Inside the Belgium pavilion at the
Shanghai Expo 2012.

Donostia – San Sebastián

When *Europe (to the power of) n* was conceived, the inclusion of Euskadi – the Basque Region in Spain that extends over France – was already settled. Its long-lasting struggle for independence (Euskadi was finally granted the status of nationality within Spain in 1979) and the hopes connected to the European Union's policy of the regions seemed to be particularly interesting for discussion in the context of a European project; although it was unclear for a while whether it should be Bilbao or Donostia – San Sebastián. Bilbao was interesting, because it hosts the Guggenheim Museum, a global museum brand, in tension with the rootedness of a much-invoked Basque identity. The final decision for Donostia – San Sebastián, the capital city of the province of Gipuzkoa, was made, because there has always been a tension between rootedness into Basque agendas and openness to the world, due to shipping in the past and tourism today. In 2016, the popular seaside resort will be the European Capital of Culture, along with Wrocław in Poland.

---

http://www.donostia.org

SAN TELMO MUSEOA

CONSTELLATION EUROPA

ASIER MENDIZABAL
Auñamendi, 2006–2010
(installation view)

San Telmo Museum,
New Wing

173

ALEKSANDER KOMAROV
Language Lessons, 2011
(installation view)

ANNIKA ERIKSSON
Wir bleiben / The Last Tenants
2011–2013

XABIER SALABERRIA
Unconscious / Conscious, 2010
(installation view)

Peio Aguirre

The current global economic downturn has made the divergences about the concept of Europe apparent. Being the problem and its solution at the same time, the old and the new Europe is discussed agonistically in its constant and indefinite reformulation. A mosaic of national and regional identities, a historical fact or a socio-economic reality, a space of cultural consensus, an asymmetric territory… Europe is more than ever the object of thorough analysis. What is the role of culture in general and that of contemporary art in particular in interpreting these conflicting representations of Europe? What is the role played by cultural institutions and museums in this process? Which are the different versions of a participatory public sphere? And above all else, what is the role of modernisation and progress in the evolution of a shared modern culture? *Constellation Europe*: this form of the constellation can, in a sense, become a real metaphor. The same way ancient peoples and civilisations decided to link the stars with imaginary lines creating virtual silhouettes all over the celestial sphere, it may be possible to think Europe as an imaginary network of arbitrary identities, which are not necessarily associated locally, but which constitute an order in the immensity of space. As in a constellation of satellites, this project in San Sebastián is part of a wider network, a point linked to other points connecting several European cities. In this constellation, which is part of an absent totality, some of the themes have been adapted to certain social issues that affect the citizens of the Basque Country: the function of cultural institutions, language and minorities, education, national identity, the negotiation with the historical past and the memory. Contemporary art incorporates all this social content and gives it back to society through the subjective view of the artists.

However, in this constellation where are the stars? The European Union flag proudly shows twelve stars, because this number is traditionally the symbol of perfection, completeness, and unity. Contrary to the popular belief, the number of stars has nothing to do with the number of the member states, and the flag does not change with the enlargement of the European Union. What the circle shows, yet, is order and unity. This is completely the opposite of what makes a constellation, which effectively means to order a seeming chaos between distant points. Open questions remain: what happened to that idea based on a Europe of regions? What is the meaning of regionalism nowadays? Is there an alternative to the form of the nation state? Is it not a return to the closed and inward nation state that anti-European populists are pushing forward, are forcing in the current weakness of the European Union? Spain offers a paradigmatic case in this regard with two burgeoning nationalisms, as the Basque and the Catalan continually threaten the integrity of the Spanish nation state form. Contradictorily, but also necessarily, the only way to achieve independence would come from that form of the nation state which is otherwise rejected.

Flyer Design by Maite Zabaleta

EUROPA

JEAN-MARIE STRAUB –
DANIÈLE HUILLET
Europa 2005, 27 Octobre,
2006

176

Europe appears as the alternative for these claims, but can we imagine ways of being and living beyond the rigid and sclerotic form of the nation state? National identity, national representations, and being part of a community form one line of the exhibition. The colourful posters by the Danish artist Lise Harlev, *My Own Country*, 2007, reflect on the ambivalent feelings towards one's country of origin and towards nationality. Her work ironically plays with populist, slogan-like rhetoric, but rather than confirming the seeming platitudes, she turns the slogans into questions addressing the reader. Asier Mendizabal's work is able to condense in a single image (or form) a complete totality. That can be found, for example, in his conceptual approach to photography in which the self-sufficient aerial image of a village turns into a metaphor for both a distinct community and a political and territorial geography with defined contours. Xabier Salaberria's installation refers to national identity represented by architecture as well as the growing awareness of the nation-state boundaries through the "exhibition" of national identities.

Another thematic line, that of language, can be found in the work of Iñaki Garmendia, Aleksander Komarov, and Katarina Zdjelar. Garmendia's work deals with linguistic and cultural translation, in this case the interpretation and translation of punk songs sung originally in Basque language by a Taiwanese rock band. Their rehearsals turn the process of appropriation into an exercise of transcoding.

IÑAKI GARMENDIA
Kolpez Kolpe, 2003
(installation view)

ASIER MENDIZABAL
Face Value, 2013

Display Elements, 2013
by Christian Teckert

Scenario Book, 2012
Book Design by Oliver Klimpel

179

KATARINA ZDJELAR
A Girl, the Sun, and an Airplane Airplane, 2007

Komarov's films and language experiments deal with the constant negotiation of identity as they offer an insight into the intricate history of his native country, Belarus. Serbian artist Katarina Zdjelar's *A Girl, the Sun, and an Airplane Airplane*, 2007, was filmed on a sound-stage in the former Enver Hoxha Museum in Tirana, Albania. The artist invited several people from the same generation to recall their knowledge of the Russian language, which was obligatory at schools for many years under the communist regime of Enver Hoxha. After the social system had changed, the knowledge of the language disappeared as well. Education, indoctrination, and the associated ideologies play an important role not only in Zdjelar's film, but also in Nils Utsi and Arvid Skauge's *Ante*, a film series about a Sami boy, who runs away from school. The school institution and its impact on the individual are also at the heart of Ane Hjort Guttu's approach. Her film about an eight-year-old boy examines his struggle for freedom and his need to question and challenge existing rules. Sven Augustijnen's film *Spectres* introduces the subject of colonialism, a subject that has been slightly overlooked in the main debates of *Europe (to the power of) n*. The film negotiates the trauma of a nation, of Belgium, and has a closer look at its colonial past using documentary language. The use of documentary features is also significant for the "video-tract" *Europa 2005 Octobre 27* by the renowned French filmmakers Danièle Huillet and Jean-Marie Straub. The short film was made in response to an assignment commemorating the Roberto Rossellini centennial, when they were asked to imagine a moment in Ingrid Bergman's character's life as played in the movie *Europa '51*. As a response, they set the scene of their radical materialist video in the conflicting banlieues of Paris to mediate the inhumane suburban planning and the difficulties of co-existence. Finally, Annika Eriksson's *Wir bleiben / The Last Tenants* depicts a Europe, that is in transition and constantly changing its form under the invisible but strong influence of capital.

OLIVER KLIMPEL
Flags, Poster-Edition, T-shirt, 2012

Artists:
Sven Augustijnen, Annika Eriksson, Iñaki Garmendia,
Ane Hjort Guttu, Lise Harlev, Oliver Klimpel,
Aleksander Komarov, Asier Mendizabal,
Jean-Marie Straub / Danièle Huillet, Xabier Salaberria,
Christian Teckert, Katarina Zdjelar

ALEKSANDER KOMAROV
Language Lessons, 2011
(detail)

Margareta Hauschild, Director Goethe-Institut Madrid

A Preliminary Note

In the very beginning of elaborating the project idea in 2008, the EU had just grown to twenty-seven members, with other countries waiting to join, while the EU Commission was already preparing its European Neighborhood policy strategies. While the global financial crisis began in 2008 on Wall Street, Europe is increasingly suffering the effects of the crisis – even after finishing the project in 2013 – with hardly an end in sight. From the outside, Europe and more so the EU may appear very confusing and the focus of the economic and cultural interest may have shifted from Europe to Asia, South America, or South Africa, but in my opinion the wider EU – including its neighbours in the north and in the south – has made an enormous progress as far as fostering its cultural and linguistic diversity are concerned. If we have a European identity, it is clearly the awareness of our diversity for which we are still willing to invest a lot of our resources.

Europe (to the power of) n in Donostia – San Sebastián was hosted by Museo San Telmo from 21 February to 21 April 2013 in "Laboratorio", the only room dedicated to contemporary art. There is no museum for contemporary art in San Sebastián currently, but the recently renovated San Telmo in the centre of the city, with its focus on archeology and ethnography, but also on painting and photography, was the perfect place for *Europe (to the power of) n.*

Situated on the Atlantic coast and bordering the Basque provinces of South-West France, San Sebastián is not only the capital of the most homogenous Basque province – besides Alava and Viscaya – it is also the number one gastronomic capital of Spain, the host of the number one Spanish film festival every mid-September, and the favourite Spanish city for many Spaniards. San Sebastián has been selected the European Cultural Capital for 2016 after a very fierce competition between many Spanish cities. I cannot think of any other place in Europe where multilingualism and cultural diversity have become everyday realities like in San Sebastián. Basque and Spanish are official languages, French as the neighbour language as well as English as a global language are omnipresent. The Basque Country has never been a melting pot. It has, on the contrary, always been a place of disharmonies and even terrorism. That is why the motto for the ECC2016 is so very important: CONVIVENCIA (co-existence).

Peio Aguirre selected twelve artistic statements, among them three by Basque artists: Iñaki Garmendia, Asier Mendizabal, and Xabier Salaberria. All of them are well known in Spain and their works are part of Spanish and Basque art collections. The opening was a gathering of literally all of the Basque artists and intellectuals to finally see and listen to the *Europe (to the power of) n* project in reality, of which they had been hearing or reading since the first scenario phase in Leipzig in 2011. The audience was very curious to discover Peio Aguirre's selection from the huge *Europe (to the power of) n* network and the interaction of the twelve very different artistic positions in San Telmo. During the four weeks, there were four dates offered to the public to meet with different artists and their works – significant encounters between Europe and the Basque Country, which will certainly have impacts for 2016 and beyond.

LISE HARLEV,
My Own Country, 2005

http://www.europe-n. org/

Collective Communication
and the *Europe^n cloud*

Christopher Köhler

Europe^n cloud

is an online communication platform. It has been developed by
an interdisciplinary team within the framework of the project
Europe (to the power of) n.[1]
The system was created in order to enable all participants to engage in
discourses related to the project and communicate them to the public.

THE PROBLEM OF CONSENSUS

The conceptual approach of *Europe (to the power of) n* is built upon a complex idea of its main subject matter. Art director Barbara Steiner writes: "An understanding of a Europe that is pluralistic, heterogeneous and frayed and full of contradictions forms the basis of the project."[2] This notion of complexity and multiplicity remains the common theme throughout all aspects of the project, be it conceptual, organisational, structural, or with regard to public communication. It produces a complex communicative situation within which the participants have to deal with the matter of consensus concerning crucial questions, such as "what is the common impulse which serves as the starting point for each participant?" and "how should this joint endeavour be communicated to the public?"

There are several different strategies to answer such questions in the context of any project. The easiest way may be to create an authority, which determines the communication policies. This authority might be put into effect by an editorial team that provides a solution based on the requirements of a successful public relations strategy and, thus, assumes the monopoly of interpretation. Alternatively, the participants could try to achieve a consensus on these matters during the planning phase of their project.

The result of either strategy is likely to be a rather consistent narrative, which represents, in essence, a transformation of multifaceted information into a homogeneous output channel. The same applies to the question about the common impulse: the outcome will likely be a valid result, a final decision, and a coherent representation from the start. However, it is evident that these approaches considerably limit the complexity of what can be communicated. Therefore, they are not suitable for a project, which tries to embody within its internal structure a "Europe [which] has challenging relationships to others, is challenged and challenges itself in itself."[3]

The *Europe (to the power of) n* project team opted for an alternative solution to the dilemma between conventions in communication and the fundamental commitment to complexity: a discursive approach.

It should allow multiple perspectives to be considered without editorial supervision, develop a platform for multi-voiced communication without authoritative definitions, and, thus, create a channel that offers information without striving for a linear narrative.

Ultimately, rather than having limited its potential through agreements made in advance, the project took the form of discourse as a way to facilitate complex communication about contingent perspectives that transcends disciplines, nation state borders, and cultural particularities. It became a forum for individual mindsets, which do not necessarily overlap. As a result, it extends the communication to a level where it is possible to speak about how to speak with one another. On this meta-level, it becomes possible to find similarities and coherences between contingent perspectives. The underlying consensus in this discourse is not an agreement about its outcome. It is the mutual agreement of all participants on their intention to communicate.

EUROPE^n CLOUD PLATFORM

In order to facilitate this challenging communication situation with its international scope *Europe^n cloud* was developed as an online platform. It is built around three major aspects: semantic structure of information, the concept of authorship, and visualisation of complexity.

SEMANTIC STRUCTURE OF INFORMATION

Fundamental to the *Europe^n cloud* concept is the assumption that the principle of speaking to one another is crucial for how information is exchanged in general. Consequently, the grammatical structure of a simple declarative sentence was chosen for all interactions on the platform: subject – predicate – object. Any information that is added can become connected to any other piece of information, which is or will be on the platform. It may be both a subject, which refers to an object, or an object, which is referred to. The connections between subjects and objects denote relations, which are directional in the sense of the grammatical structure of the declarative sentence.

Much like in spoken and written language, the predicate constitutes additional information about the subject and the object as it indicates their relation and, thus, the structure they are part of. In *Europe^n cloud,* this superstructure is built by applying this simple grammatical principle to all pieces of information. As a result, a network is produced, which is a rendition of the complex interrelations of the information exchange on a data level.

CONCEPT OF AUTHORSHIP

Any piece of information is contributed by a certain author. It is not limited to a particular form, either technically or communicatively. Texts and images as well as data files and external links, or a combination of these different formats, can be articulations and serve, for instance, as arguments or commentaries.

Independent of their actual function, all pieces of information are regarded as statements by their author to whom they remain unmistakably linked. There are two important consequences, which result from this idea. One is that there is no predefined logic of how content has to be published. Instead, all authors can articulate themselves with their individual voice and in the way, which makes most sense to them. There are no systematic regulations besides the technological necessities for using the online platform. The other consequence is that there is no notion of truth, which is established and sustained by any kind of formal institution. Without editorial supervision any viewpoint can be introduced into the evolving content network and contribute to its discourses.

Furthermore, the organisational structure of *Europe (to the power of) n* does not dictate any

limitations to who may use the platform. Everyone involved in the project can gain access. All authors who participate do so on an equal level and, thus, have the same opportunities. They are able to participate with a variety of goals and approaches, such as interests in different perspectives, acquiring alternative standpoints, introducing themselves as well as contributing to the network and experimenting with the communicative possibilities. This unrestricted access to collective communication distinctly shapes the content structure. The platform's content is argumentative instead of explanatory. It accumulates information about a topic rather than exhausting it. Composed of individual knowledge that is shared among equal partners, the outcome is a meaningful randomness.

This approach to collective communication has a tendency towards an overabundance of information. Hence, the third of the major aspects in developing the *Europe^n cloud* platform is the visualisation of its content.

VISUALISATION OF COMPLEXITY

The complex network of information generated through publishing content requires efficient tools, which enable users to access and read it. For that purpose, *Europe^n cloud* provides a user interface. Its visualisations are essentially abstract graphical translations of the content and, consequently, based on the same grammatical structure. Therefore, the superstructure, which is composed of the interrelations between particular pieces of information, is the starting point for the reception process. The visualisation designs enable each user to navigate through the structure, determine the displayed data, and preview and access the underlying information level at any moment during the interaction. Furthermore, there is the option to display an overview of the whole content structure and, thus, gain a completely new perspective on the discourse. Evidently, the process of reception, of reading content on *Europe^n cloud,* is highly individual. Without a predefined direction or any linear, moderated sequence, as is typical for conventional texts, it is possible for recipients to explore the platform according to their particular interests and intentions.

1 Members of the *Europe^n cloud* development team throughout the *Europe (to the power of) n* project have been: Konrad Abicht, Vanessa Boni, Andrea Hribernik, Christopher Köhler, Tristan Schulze, and Barbara Steiner. The platform can be accessed online on http://www.europe-n.org/

2 http://www.europe-n.org/site/show/frame/pid/270 (access: January 3, 2013)

3 Ibid.

Visualisations of the *Europe^n cloud* database
Design by Tristan Schulze, 2012
(screenshots)

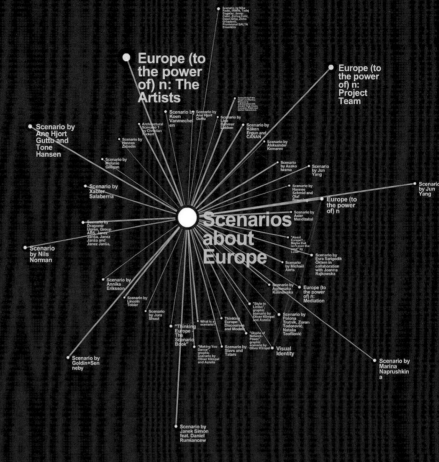

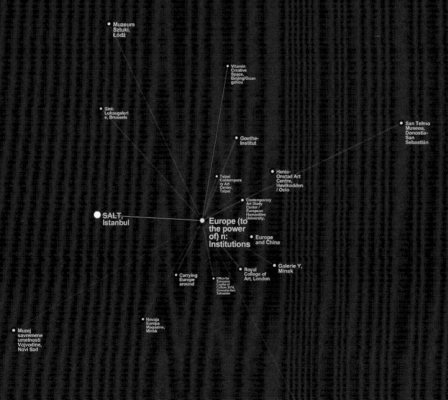

As a result, there is a high degree of autonomy on the part of the individual users regarding the process and progress of their interaction with the system. Each one constructs her or his own narrative and, hence, assumes a unique monopoly of interpretation of what is relevant and what is not. The sole defining element of the communicative situation into which the user enters is his or her willingness to interact with the system and acquire information. This strongly correlates with the authors's consensus about their intention to communicate, as every publication includes the connection of one's own content to that of others and, therefore, requires the author to simultaneously assume the role of the recipient. Conversely, it seems only logical that, eventually, the platform will cease to be a means which is used to communicate a singular project to the public. It has to be opened up so recipients can join in and actively be authors of their individual perspective, which is in itself part of the multiplicity that is fundamental to the discourse about Europe.

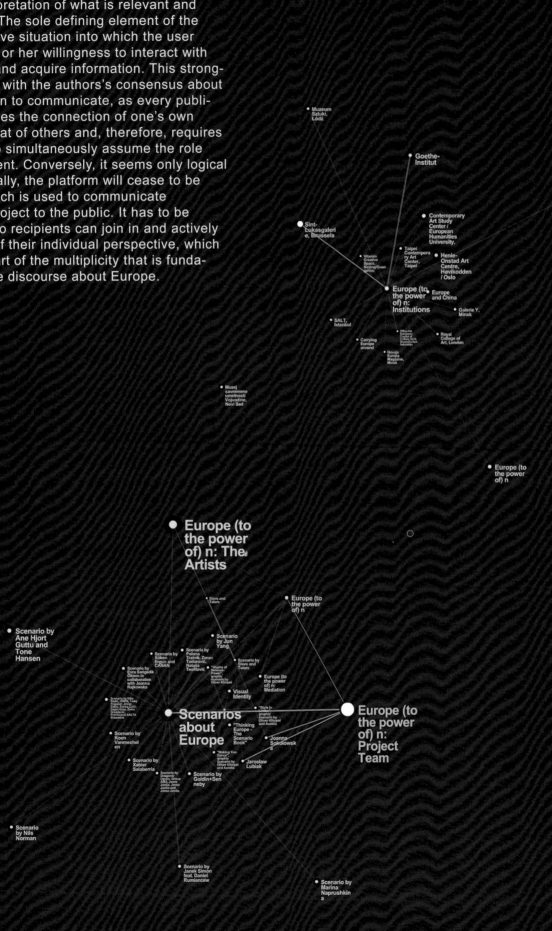

189

L'ÉLÉMENT

CHRISTIAN TECKERT: As expected, the level of interest in engaging in a dialogue about the spatial settings as a potential arena of this architectural contribution within *Europe (to the power of) n* varied a lot. But this was also part of the concept insofar as there was a wide range of possible forms of engagement embedded in this contribution. In order to allow this variety, we prepared a "manual" for the curators to communicate the options that exist within this rather flexible architectural system. Based on three elements – a line, a surface, an object – we tried to offer some very basic elements for display techniques as a kind of toolbox.

CT: In these cities, the whole range of our elements was also realised and integrated into the exhibition settings, while in other cases – like in İstanbul or in Minsk – only one specific aspect of the architectural elements was realised. Seen together, these differences in dealing with a given framework representing a kind of meta-structure also create a "portrait" of the specific interests and agendas connected to specific curatorial or institutional practices. The architectural concept basically defined as a "toolbox" also allowed differences, ambivalences, and incongruences between those practices to become visible. However, the hope of this toolbox being a possible site of ongoing debate about the role of the spatial setting in exhibitions and their politics of display was maybe a bit too high.

A Portrait of Specific Interests and Agendas

Invitation for the exhibition in London, July 2012, designed by Kit Hammonds

OLIVER KLIMPEL: Compared to *Scenarios about Europe,* for the graphic identity of the project *Europe (to the power of) n* I pursued the idea of a much more individualised response to the partners involved. It was important to me to challenge very clearly branding for cultural institutions in the current mould. In that sense, I suppose, we both shared an attempt for a practical discourse or inquiry into the role of graphics and architecture, respectively, in the arena of exhibitions or art spaces. On the other hand, it seemed crucial to me to operate with an approach that suggested interaction, but most importantly was not dependent on many elements. Interaction was welcome, but the approach was deliberately not too reliant on a high level of participation to make it work. For the visual identity I opted for an unconventional sibling logo situation, which was simultaneously open and solid and could be applied very easily. This visual sign was not definite, but by the same token it was very easy to use. It did not impose any restrictions on the users; it did not require specific skills or extra efforts. It was a deliberate move to work with a near absence of rules. The logo was its own cliché, in the sense of an imprint. And on the other hand, there the concept allowed for very bespoke and unique design contributions, which I would develop with the curators who were interested in that, and who would be interested in a collaboration that was specific to this project, rather than sticking to their normal institutional set-up, or merge the two. In London, Novi Sad, and Beijing it was like this.

OK: In collaborations, there are plenty of reasons why things happen or do not happen. The famous Karl Valentin quote comes to mind: "Kunst ist schön, macht aber viel Arbeit" ("art is beautiful but hard work"). This is the practical problem of collaboration. However, it is a matter of control, too. As soon as there is miscommunication about certain things, if there is emphasis on an efficient and result-driven approach, collaboration – with a certain level of the unknown and unexpected – starts to get complicated. I have always looked at this as being very interesting in regards to the design; I like these lost-in-translation situations, particularly in this project, which I tried to treat differently to most others. Some misunderstandings were rather welcome. However, this means leaving the comfort zone of a certain idea of quality that one has. Some of the design produced at the various venues certainly was at odds with graphics I would favour, but I thought it conceptually very crucial to have precisely these various ideas of what graphics should do as part of the project: either being produced by me or others. It requires a step aside from the notion of quality one usually applies, and actually requires renegotiating what quality could be.

Whose domain is it and what was imposed?

OK: As I just pointed out, I did not feel like imposing a very high concept of structural principle, which would be easily understandable but heavily restrictive: something I did not feel was that interesting. Yes, it would have bound things more neatly together, but I was completely happy letting things go at certain moments. I think in comparison to the architectural principle, which is rather structural, it was more open.

CT: Probably it looked more restrictive than it was, or to put it differently, it was strict in its conception but not in its application. In addition to the inherent variability of the architectural concept as a "toolbox", where you could choose some elements from, there was a also predictable tendency to appropriate the "rules" defined in the "manual" and interpret them in different ways. However, in some cases it seemed that in order to avoid any "improper" element within the specific curatorial decisions the presence of an overarching project was minimised or at some points ignored. I guess this also speaks of a general tendency in contemporary curating, where after exhibition formats have been deconstructed and experimented with to an extent that the permanent questioning – especially of spatial preconditions of exhibiting – has become almost formalism.

Invitation for the exhibition in Łódź, September 2012, designed by Jakub de Barbaro

E-mail-flyer for the exhibition in Høvikodden / Oslo, November 2012, designed by Eriksen / Brown

OK: I think that's an interesting point. The project very much succeeded in highlighting some issues or, say, gaps that have emerged between the discourse of curatorial practice and the practice of curating in the context of the priorities, hierarchies, and methods. The project is most definitely as much about the state of contemporary progressive curating and its institutional implications as it is about the idea of Europe. It just seems, even though exhibitions are such a wide field, there is a clear focus on the idea of art and artistic positions within an exhibition format. It raised the questions of the role of the institution as a frame, and design and architecture as devices to provide these critical frames. If you look at the history of the exhibitions from the 1930s with Alfred Barr up to the end of the 1970s at MOMA, as it is very convincingly presented in Staniszewski's book *The Power of Display*, you can see how visual and spatial design were absolutely integral and useful tools to reflect the role and politics of displays in an art space as well as facilitating the viewing of works of fine art. And then there is a cut in the late 1970s, roughly, when all of a sudden the discursive power of design is gone and completely delegated solely to the artist whose practice has an interest in these questions of display. And this is a tendency one can still find in many art institutions, many of them with an immense reputation: a lack of institutional culture of pursuing or tackling these issues through practice with works that are not themselves implicated in the art market, namely design and architecture. But this is not specific to our project.

CT: Maybe you could also say that the critical impact of many former transgressive avant-garde practices has been slowly but steadily incorporated into the activities and conventions of contemporary curating exemplified by the debate on "new institutionalism". Diverse forms of participation, mediation, workshops, role-play and so on have steadily altered and expanded the framework of exhibiting, so that the

Poster for the exhibition in Novi
Sad, November 2012, designed
by Mira Dušić

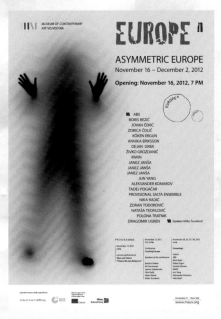

A European Exhibition Space,
collage of various Europeⁿ venues,
in a straight line, by Christian Teckert
and Christine Bock

Questioning of the singular exhibition negotiations

curatorial position increasingly designs, creates, and controls this complex framework. I think that in this development, new conventions were also created, where especially graphic and architectural design became also a more instrumental aspect of curatorial positions, and on the other hand thereby became maybe less autonomous and less powerful. In my opinion, the attitude towards such a comprehensive layer like the question of display embedded within *Europe (to the power of) n* speaks of two related problems: on the one hand, the spatial setting of an exhibition is often considered as the sole domain of curatorial decisions, where articulations other than artworks find no proper place; and on the other hand, there might also be a general precaution at play against an "imposed" architectural agenda coming from this rather abstract realm of a meta-structure representing maybe a similar problem as the legal powers of the EU represent for the inividual interests of singular nations. Taking this into consideration, I think both the architectural concept as well as the graphic and visual identity for *Europe (to the power of) n* tried to engage in an attempt to create platforms for articulating these questions, but were positioned structurally in a situation of being a surplus, sometimes a welcome or rather unwelcome disturbance.

OK: I was really surprised that there was not more use made of the incredible freedom within the project. In other words, that there were not more alternative formats than the traditional exhibition. It tells us something about our professions or the expectations and conventions that determine which way of making arguments feels comfortable to us, or promises the right kind of academic legacy. It tells us more about problems of progressive curatorial practice today than about design in collaborative processes.

CT: Generally speaking, I see the most interesting aspect of this form of collaborating in the necessity to think of exhibitions as temporary, provisional, and also highly personal settings defined by different curatorial intentions. By working in a structure defined by a succession of scenarios, discussions, conferences, Internet-based communication, and publications – as it was the case of the *Europe (to the power of) n* project – the status of the singular exhibition as the final and crucial articulation basically could be questioned in many ways.

193

Invitation and poster for the exhibition in Minsk, September 2012, designed by Jura Shust

Invitation and leaflet for the exhibition in Donostia – San Sebastián, February 2013, designed by Maite Zabaleta

Invitation for the exhibition in Brussels, February 2013

OK: But why then was there an occasionally surprising emphasis on autonomy in regards to spatial and graphic design in a few cases? Is it purely down to making the production process more efficient, less of a time-consuming dialogue? Was it about not "ruffling too many feathers", an unfamiliarity about the discourses of design and architecture, matters of taste, power or just sheer disagreement? I am occasionally amused by the discrepancies between the reality of a project like this and the things that appear in essays, which are always big pleas for multiplicity, fluidity, and exchange. And then, as soon as there is a chance to actually put some of these things into practice, one withdraws to routines which are less exhausting, or a much easier way of going about it and not losing focus, because as someone planning an exhibition or any other format you want to choose your battles, so maybe this is not the one you feel the urge to engage in …

Typography of entrance wall in the exhibition in London, July 2012, designed by Kit Hammonds

SHARED RESPONSIBILITY

KIT HAMMONDS: The architectural concept Christian had developed probably provoked more debate from the curators. If one followed his proposals completely, the three design elements were quite invasive on the exhibitions as a whole and on the space, or, one could say, autonomy of the works of art. In London, he ended up having more impact than originally planned. When planning and installing I thought, "oh, actually now that could work there quite nicely. Oh great! Let's do that!". Originally, I tried to modify the proposals and thought of drawing the one-metre line on the windows but in the end we carried out the original proposal of a pencil line – it seemed an unnecessary compromise that made Christian's proposal more present somehow. On the gallery walls, however, the line was used as a baseline for the labels.
With Oliver, I thought his pared-down branding was really interesting, because it had an acknowledgement of a corporate relationship that branding has to public space and shared space. And I wanted to build within this a workspace that allowed me to have a conversation with the security guard and people within some kind of setting. So I set the scene and asked, "why don't we take the design and rather than use it to brand the exhibition let us brand the space in the exhibition". That actually was a very organic thing; originally at the start I did not really know what to do with Oliver's design, because it was quite a different approach to design. I normally work with a designer on a basis of a brief. I had not really understood that the design element was another position like artists or curators have. And that is why I think I wanted to incorporate it more as a position within the show, rather than an offer of some design elements I can take or reject. This was the reason I put both names, Oliver's and Christian's, on the invitations alongside the artists.

WRONG CONTEXT

LENA PRENTS: Why Guggenheim colours? It seemed overformalistic to me and felt inappropriate in relation to the context of my exhibition in Minsk. To divide walls horizontally – as it was the case with the benchmark line – and to paint them in pastel colours is paralleled to a lot of former and existing design of public buildings in Belarus like hospitals, schools, administrations. In addition, museums in Belarus overuse colours in their exhibition spaces. Given that, had I used the Guggenheim colours, it would have been important to develop a counter-model to the existing models. But it is difficult to look for a good solution without a strong inner belief. Furthermore, it was not easy to mediate the project and the contents of the exhibition. So I decided to focus more on the artworks and less on the frames of presentation. Nevertheless, I tried to realise the minimum, which was possible: the one-metre benchmark line, and Oliver, who was there, devised a way of showing his edition of poster-prints. One day, such projects strongly engaged with the frames of presentation will be possible I am sure; especially in Belarus where we still face a strong concentration on the formal qualities of the artwork and less on the frames surrounding it. Maybe then it will raise a new debate on formalism.

A TOOL FOR MEDIATION

JOANNA SOKOŁOWSKA: At the beginning, we perceived Christian Teckert's units as kind of strange element and we did not really know what it was. It took us a while until we knew what to do with them.

JAROSŁAW LUBIAK: They are sort of formalistic …

JS: For me a big problem was that Jarosław and I were part of the *Europe (to the power of) n* project, but the local audience was not engaged in the common agenda and there were some levels of the common formats, which might be only visible and understandable for people who participated in our network. We discussed several ideas with Krzysztof Skoczylas, our architect for the exhibition, and he came up with some good proposals for how to mediate Christian's proposal in our location. He decided to incorporate the benchmark line to his walls constructed for the exhibition: up to the one-metre benchmark height, the walls were covered and painted white, whereas the zone above was semi-transparent and made of unpainted wooden boards. While the lower part of the wall looked completed, the zone above appeared like it was under construction. The construction of the walls turned into the leading motif of the exhibition display. I think the benchmark division did not attract much attention; the most tangible effect of the exhibition architecture was that of the dynamic, shifting, and multiple perspectives, from which to view particular artworks and to establish links between them.

JL: Krzysztof's first idea was also to have different Guggenheim colours in the exhibition but it was too much. It would not have worked with the artworks. Therefore, we ended up with two colours, which were used for the walls that displayed information about the exhibition.

JS: We eventually used the shelves for workshops and we put them in the entrance area, close to the bookshop. They were covered with some items from the workshops, books and texts related to the exhibition.

JL: Our education team used the units as a tool. They invited people – kids mostly – to fill them. It became a tool for mediation.

INTRICACIES

LARA FRESKO: It was very hard to explain the entire *Europe (to the power of) n* project to SALT: I had difficulties explaining all the intricacies, the role of the partners involved, what had happened before and what was going to happen in İstanbul. It would have become more difficult with the common formats. I have

never met Christian and Oliver. I should have, perhaps, made more of an effort, however, I was not sure to what extent these components were supposed to be integral to the entire project. I had not really looked at how they had worked with Kit – if I had known, perhaps I would have made more of an effort to involve them.
ESRA SARIGEDIK ÖKTEM: The meetings in Leipzig and Berlin were really an important part of the project and unfortunately I could only attend two of them and then I had to pause because of my baby. Lara joined the project later on but did never meet our colleagues. This was a problem, too.
LF: I think it was important that Christine came and this is why her component really worked well. And I think Christian did very well in letting her do it, because she had already seen the space, she knew about the whole situation. Generally speaking I think Esra's curatorial vision for this whole project was very tight, it made great sense in and of itself, and so I think in any case it was very hard to place something inside this which was not there from the very beginning.
ESÖ: Well, one of the problems was that we were too focused on potential technical issues how to realise Oliver's and Christian's proposals. However, I think it was mainly the missing communication between us, SALT, Oliver, and Christian. Actually, it was a conceptual problem. But I am realising this just now. When we got their proposals it was already too late to develop ideas on how to deal with them.

IRONIC, NOT CRITICAL

TONE HANSEN: I think the common formats brought the projects together and allowed for the heterogeneity of the project to come through. Within Europe (to the power of) n, we worked with very different institutional formats – this has also become visible through the common formats. And I love Christians Teckert's Euro-pallet, as it resembles the logic of the EU for me – bureaucratic, economic – which is also suppressive in its limiting form. I just had a problem with the use of the Guggenheim colours, because for me this was something that was added in the midst of a collaborative project without having gone through an open discussion at first. For me, it became superficial in the way it was implemented, and as a critique of the Guggenheim Empire it failed. This would have required more articulation. As an artistic project I think it could have been very interesting, but not as a rule everybody has to follow. My opinion is that it became ironic, not critical, and apart from this it would have been very difficult to explain to my audience what it was and what it did in our exhibition.

CIRCULATION OF IDEAS

MIŠKO ŠUVAKOVIĆ: For me, it was interesting to see how the ideas from a designer grounded in the British-German contexts would adjust to the Serbian context. When I saw Oliver Klimpel's solution for the catalogue layout for the first time I was a little bit angry. From my point of view, it looked very bad – too asymmetric and unfinished. But when Oliver, Dragomir Ugren, who was his collaboration partner in Novi Sad, and I discussed the concept I got the idea and then it became very useful for me, because I took it as a formula of asymmetry for the realisation of the Novi Sad exhibition, and this means that the book cover was translated back to the exhibition display. Finally, the catalogue and the exhibition in Novi Sad are forms of circulation of the word "asymmetric" which was suggested to me by Barbara Steiner three years ago. First, the idea of "asymmetry" circulated between her and me, then between Oliver, Ugren, and me. The event of circulating ideas has become more important than the representation of image or the installation itself. It shows how concepts turn into human conditions in every specific relation between curators, designer and artists. When I met Christian for the first time in Leipzig, I did not know what he exactly wanted with his concept. In the last few months, I was working with a few architects from Belgrade. They spoke about how architectural elements or sets of such elements circulate in different contexts. And then I was able to connect this with Christian's ideas, and when he sent me these drawings I really looked at them carefully for the first time. Then I started to think that it could be very useful to have something like this in the Novi Sad exhibition. When Christine Bock, his collaboration partner, came she spent two-and-a-half days in Novi Sad, but I could only be there for one day, because I was totally busy with lectures. She asked me what she could do. I said, "just decide". She grasped the opportunity immediately and decided. Finally, we moved artworks according to her suggestions. I only asked for a shelf for IRWIN's magazines because they did not want to have them on the walls. For me it was the perfect solution. Finally, all things were connected and in circulation – not only regarding Christian and Oliver's work, but also when it came to the art production. Take Ugren as an example: he responded to the scenarios period in Leipzig and made a drawing, which imagined his presentation there. This drawing was placed opposite the shelves Christine put up, together with his large paintings, oscillating in between design, architecture, painting, surface, and space. On a very abstract level of construction, they corresponded perfectly well. Ideas and things circulate: this is what I am interested in.

CONFLICTING WITH ARTISTIC PRESENTATIONS

FILIP LUYCKX: On first consideration, it could be interesting to trace a red thread running through all the *Europe (to the power of) n* exhibitions through the presence of architectural and design elements. To function in at least eight exhibitions at once, those forms and signs have to assume, by necessity, the role of abstract bodies in any particular exhibition. In my opinion, additional elements may only be considered as relevant contributions if they cohere within the context of the exhibition. The visual presentation of the exhibition is the

logical result of a deep involvement with the concept, knowledge of the displayed artworks, dialogue with the artists, acquaintance with the given architecture,
and rules of the three exhibition venues in Brussels. That means that a whole
process precedes the installation of the exhibition. At the various European
venues, there were constraints with regards to either the content of the work, the
use of the architecture, or the technical facilities. The artists were informed about
them and demonstrated a huge flexibility towards this situation. The available
rooms were huge, but we gradually learned that the different rules substantially
reduced the useable space. Only at the final point of this process did the
pre-existent architectural and design elements arrive. What is their status in the
midst of the dialogue between the artworks, the competition with the rather
disturbing institutional signage and furniture, and the omnipresent installation
rules? Placed at the entrance of the exhibition, they could make a connection to
the European frame, but inside the exhibition space itself the architectural
elements would have been in conflict with a carefully constructed presentation.

DISPLAY AS A KEY APPROACH

PEIO AGUIRRE: I could easily integrate the common formats into my exhibition
and I had no problems including Oliver and Christian's names in the artist list.
For some curators, this might be a problem and artists are often critical about
this, too. They do not want to see their names aligned with, say, a kind of "meta-
conceptual applied art" or a variant of functionalism. My view of the common
formats is that they are needed to highlight that the single projects are part of
Europe (to the power of) n – in my case to show that Constellation Europa is a
site-specific project, exhibition, and screening programme, which is part of a
larger structure. The one-metre line and the Euro-pallet had their own function in
the show. To use the line was an aesthetic and spatial decision. Because it was
used on all temporary walls, it somehow connected the various parts of the
exhibition. However, one aspect Christian proposed did not make sense to me:
to stick to a colour selection from the Guggenheim colour charts. In my opinion,
it would have been easier and more pragmatic to take the Natural Colour
System (NCS), which is a more universal guide for colours. The Guggenheim
colours presuppose that museums need a specific palette for the display of
masterpieces. However, a much more dynamic contemporary art field does not
require this kind of classicism. In regards to the graphic design, one challenge
was to distinguish information about the exhibition or an artwork from the
artworks themselves, although in Aleksander Komarov's vinyl text both aspects
overlap: it is information and part of the artwork at the same time. "Display" is a
key term in my approach. Within such an approach Oliver Klimpel's poster-
edition, the book, and the Europe T-shirt make sense next to the graphic design
of Maite Zabaleta, with whom I have worked on the occasion of this project in
San Sebastián.

TESTING GROUND

JUN YANG: One of the appeals of participating in *Europe (to the power of) n*
was the approach of looking at both the content and the working method from
a different perspective: not a horizontal working method but a combination
of curators, architects, designers, and artists. One could also say if Europe is
a model of how individual identities can co-exist and work together on different
levels, then perhaps *Europe (to the power of) n* was also a model or testing
ground for the way in which different individuals within contemporary art and
cultural production can work together and create an exhibition series with
multiple levels. For me, this is an interesting approach or counter-model to the
existing "megalomania biennial" exhibition model. Therefore, I was also
interested to have Christian and Oliver involved as early as possible. I had
already tested this collaboration in Leipzig by inviting them to come up with a
scenario for a potential exhibition in Beijing.

POSTSCRIPT

CHRISTINE BOCK: By being directly involved in the exhibitions in London,
İstanbul, Novi Sad, and Brussels and being on site for their installation,
I experienced different types of collaboration, interests, and parameters, which
implied a challenge for the integration of the architectural contribution. Yet at the
same time, the integration became a tool to reveal these conditions and
challenges.
It seemed that all participants involved in the projects, including myself, had
sometimes very different, even opposing expectations, interests, and goals depending on their roles as artists, curators, architects, or as someone who acts on
behalf of the institution. By integrating architectural elements within the exhibitions, communication between the parties became a necessity, and in this way
different expectations could be revealed and negotiations between positions
could be initiated. In the case of the Brussels exhibition, which took place in the
European quarter, in the building of the European Economic and Social Committee and of the Committee of the Regions, one of Christian's shelving units
was placed on the windowsill marginal to the exhibition. This decision was made
in consideration of the restrictive rules of the institution and to avoid competition
with the artworks. The architectural contribution was, therefore, neither integrated nor made use of: the absence of the architectural concept and the failed
communication were visible. In the end, the strength of the architectural
scenarios depended rather on the way in which the initiated negotiation and its
challenges were inscribed in the placement and integration of the elements than
on its use.

Beijing

Taipei

China's participation in this project is to be understood in an exemplary way.[1] If a project about Europe had been carried out in the 1950s or 1960s, the emphasis would have most probably been placed on its relations with the United States in the West, and with the Soviet Union in the East. Today, the relationship between "Europe" and the People's Republic of China can be described as more exposed in comparison to other relationships to non-European countries. This exposed relationship is reflected not only by media coverage, but also by political, economic, and cultural undertakings. At first sight, the People's Republic of China – assertive and economically success-ful – seems to be the opposite model to Europe seen as a frayed, inherently contradictory congeries. However, there are a lot of debates doubting the Peoples Republic of China's homogeneity, and there are a lot of debates addressing the directive "One country, many systems".[2] In continuation of these debates Taiwan was invited as it challenges China's image of a great, homogenous, and stable block just as the first mentioned places; Brussels, İstanbul, London, Łódź, Minsk, Novi Sad, Oslo, and Donostia – San Sebastián challenge the idea of a strong "core" Europe from the perspective of the periphery.

1   However, the relationship between "Europe" and China/Taiwan is not the only point of interest: within *Europe (to the power of) n* the works of art set Europe in relation to others. Exemplary positions are Janek Simon's Polish Mission in Auroville, who connects to India, and Slavs and Tatars's project *Reverse Joy*, which connects to the Arabic world.

2   Today the People's Republic of China conceives itself as a unity that is multi-fold, endorsed by the directive: "One country, many systems". Some years after Hong Kong joined the People's Republic of China this directive, which once had addressed Hong Kong and other special economic areas, was not seen as a possibility to guarantee a unified country, but to allow different systems under one umbrella. This model has also been discussed as an appropriate solution for Taiwan. Lu Ping, *Fünf ungewöhnliche Jahre*, July 2002 http://www.chinatoday.com.cn/chinaheute/207/7w1.htm, 22 December 12

VITAMIN CREATIVE SPACE,
BEIJING

TAIPEI
CONTEMPORARY
ART CENTER

AND

ARTCO MONTHLY

Does Europe Matter?

Jun Yang

Does Europe matter? followed the ideas sketched out in *Scenarios about Europe,* the exhibition series preceding *Europe (to the power of) n.* Finally, all three scenarios: a weekend conference, a magazine, and an exhibition were carried out with some adaptation. After the magazine *Art World* dropped out completely, the magazine was conceived by the Taipei Contemporary Art Center and a Chinese version was published in collaboration with the Taipei-based art magazine *Artco Monthly*. The conference, the presentation of the magazine, and the exhibition were put together and presented at *The Pavilion* (Vitamin Creative Space) in Beijing in April 2013.

Within *Europe (to the power of) n,* my concept proposed looking at Europe from the outside, not only from a remote geographical standpoint, but also from a different cultural perspective. What is Europe? Where does Europe start? Which countries belong to the EU and which ones do not? Is there a European identity or a European identity crisis? All these problems and discussions currently taking place in Europe become ponderous as soon as one looks at the construction of Europe from a distant perspective. Does Europe matter in Europe or in China? Compared to other relationships the positioning of Europe in China seemed to be significant, and the most interesting at this moment. *Does Europe matter?* examined these questions and created a dialogue between artists, curators, and scholars from the project *Europe (to the power of) n* and colleagues from China, Hong Kong, and Taiwan.

The following pages show the site,
The Pavilion, and the first preparations for
the exhibition and conference.

Since the opening and the conference were planned for the 5 and 6 April and this book went to the printer on 3 April, it is not possible to show installation shots or to document the conference. However, the focus on "what might be" supports imaginations and speculations about the relationship between China and Europe, which is most challenging but nevertheless incredibly vague, at least seen against the background of current debates.

e (preliminary)
03. 03. 2013

策划人 Curated by
胡昉 Fang Hu
Barbara Steiner
Jun Yang

视觉设计 Visuals
Oliver Klimpel

空间设计 Architecture
Christian Teckert

场地 Venue:
观心亭 the pavilion
(((维他命空间)))(((vitamin creative space)))

地址:
朝阳区百子湾路32号苹果社区北区2号楼B座2503
Address:
2503-B-Building 2,
Northern District,
Pingod Community,
No. 32 Baiziwan Road, Chaoyang District,
Beijing, CHINA

Europe^n
ne Mood for Love

http://www.europe-n.org
http://site.douban.com/theshop/
http://www.vitamincreativespace.com/

GOETHE
INSTITUT

Allianz
Kulturstiftung

欧洲^n
七样年华

Vitamin Creative Space

Poster by Oliver Klimpel, 2012
(developed for *Scenarios about Europe*). The title of the exhibition has meanwhile changed.

Does Europe matter? marked the end of a series of exhibitions within the framework of *Europe (to the power of) n*. Thus, both the exhibition and the conference gave the people involved a chance not only to look at the project from a distant point of view, but also to re-examine and reflect upon the series of exhibitions that took place at the respective locations. For this reason, all the curators of *Europe (to the power of) n* were invited to choose one artwork from their exhibitions as both a contribution to the Chinese exhibition and as a link to their own project and its location. The shown artworks were reproductions: no "original" was displayed. As much as the entire exhibition was a thumbnail of all previous manifestations, the artworks on display were copies as well.

205

THE PAVILION

The Pavilion in Beijing sits on top of an office/apartment high-rise. It is a cubed shaped loft space on the 25th floor, located in the business district (3rd ring) of Beijing. It was created by Vitamin Creative Space in order to initiate a platform rather than a classical exhibition venue, which aims at not only testing forms of presentation, but asking what a space of contemporary art can be today. Vitamin Creative Space is more interested in creating exchange and dialogue than in purely presenting "art". Therefore, The Pavilion's emphasis is not put on classical exhibition display, it does not have openings or a strict duration of exhibition. It never closes for the installation of the next presentation, but always remains an "open space". Even during special events, such as dinner parties, the public is welcome and can join at any moment. Last year The Pavilion installed a kitchen in its main space – starting several events around cooking, hosting dinners, and encouraging exchange and dialogue through this means. Vitamin Creative Space considers The Pavilion as a "living space", a space in progress that "breathes".

欧洲重要嗎？ 一個論壇，一本雜誌，一個展覽

欧洲重要吗？ 一个论坛，一本杂志，一个展览

THE MAGAZINE

While looking at Europe from a distant point of view – in this case from China – it was appropriate not to fix the view on "China" as one territory or one identity, but rather to include "other" Chinas: Taiwan and Hong Kong in order to incorporate another perspective and to question the notion of a "union". Looking at the concept of territories as well as at cultural and national identity from various positions, it felt interesting in the context of doing a project about Europe to address multiple "Chinas" rather than one homogeneous China.

A Chinese version of the magazine was realised in collaboration with the Taipei-based art magazine *Artco Monthly* in its April 2013 issue. The entire magazine, both the Chinese and English part, was produced as a free download, which could be printed on demand. It aimed to reflect on the Internet as a sharing and distributing platform. The magazine was edited by Meiya Cheng of the Taipei Contemporary Art Center and designed by Oliver Klimpel, responsible for the visual identity of *Europe (to the power of) n.*

Does Europe matter? was mainly nurtured by my own artistic interest and practice. Therefore, the Beijing exhibition was not about how Chinese or Beijing-based artists look at Europe, but more about subjects and issues connected to the relationship of China and Europe, filtered through my personal experience of having lived in both cultures. In collaboration with Vitamin Creative Space, the Taipei Contemporary Art Center, the magazine *Artco Monthly*, and the curators of *Europe (to the power of) n,* I looked into the relationship of China and Europe from various perspectives promoting a level of exchange beyond large representational projects.

THE CONFERENCE

The conference reflected on the relationship of "Europe" with China and the inner-relations within China. The focus was put on reading Hong Kong, Taiwan, and Mainland China in relation to one another and in relation to Europe. Colonial and post-colonial issues were addressed in equal measure. In addition, the project *Europe (to the power of) n* was debated. As its final venue was Beijing, the conference aimed at looking at Europe not only from a distant point of view but also at *Europe (to the power of) n* from a distant perspective.

Besides the questions already mentioned, some of the conference topics evolved around chances and possibilities of today's contemporary art and art initiatives in current economical and political contexts. It asked what is the social potential of contemporary art in Europe and China seen against the background of a multipolar world, and which roles do art institutions, fairs, and magazines play in mediating art to a broader audience. What is the situation of institutions in China and Europe? What can China and "Europe" learn from each other? The gathering in Beijing tried to create a platform for an exchange about different approaches ranging from local to global perspectives.

ABOUT THE FORMATION OF EUROPE (TO THE POWER OF) N

Barbara Steiner:
Looking back, the long planning period for this project is striking. Altogether, it took more than three years to implement the projects in the different locations. At the end of 2008 Sabine and I got to know one another. The parties first met in 2010, even though the final team was not confirmed until February 2011; with our practical considerations we started in September 2011.

Ilina Koralova:
I remember that we actually wanted to submit our EU application in Autumn 2010, but very soon we realised that we could not give any precise details. Although we had all the partners on board, the detailed concept still had to be developed. The institutions were also reluctant to make any binding commitments, because they did not know what their situation would be in 2012.

Sabine Hentzsch:
From today's point of view, these difficulties are not surprising: the partners would have to make a commitment and at the same time take on the obligation to take part in the co-financing. There is no institution that would readily enter into a project two years before the actual project begins. And in order to dive into detailed conceptual planning, we had to extend the planning phase. I think it was an important decision. With *Scenarios about Europe*, we allowed ourselves to think about and to play through different alternatives of how to implement a European project. Luckily, this period of extensive planning and testing was not only financed by the Goethe-Institut but also by the Cultural Foundation of Saxony.

IK: I think this phase was so important, because it strengthened the idea of collaboration. If you want to work with someone, clearly, the results of that collaboration cannot be planned in advance. However, to make an EU funding application, the outcome needs to be known in principle. I think the question of trust is crucial for this kind of project. In the beginning, we did not know everyone well enough and they did not know us well enough to enter into a project like this easily. This level of trust was reached much later. In that regard, Leipzig was a very important phase of trust-building.

BS: What I consider to be most difficult was presenting the project to potential financial backers. Very often I was told that the project was far too complicated. Therefore, it is all the more remarkable that we had success with the Robert Bosch Foundation, the European Union, and the Allianz Cultural Foundation. Luckily, Arend Oetker also helped and supported our artistic projects at the festival in Berlin. However, one major application failed. So it was quite challenging to start the project lacking the essential means we had originally been expecting.

IK: But still, it has ultimately led to a very positive development. The co-organisers – the Curating Contemporary Art Programme at the Royal College of Art in London, the Muzeum Sztuki in Łódź, the Henie-Onstad Kunstsenter in Høvikodden, and the Office for European Capital of Culture 2016 in Donostia – San Sebastián – all increased their financial commitment. Initially, they wanted to make a relatively small contribution to the overall project, and they could have easily said, "we agreed to this amount of money, and that is all we are willing to give". The fact that they significantly increased their share made our project finally possible.

SH: That is absolutely remarkable, because it shows that during the course of *Europe (to the power of) n*, people became more and more convinced by the project. Finally they decided that it was important to them, and after taking another look at their finances they were willing to give more money.

BS: Well, Høvikodden / Oslo increased their contribution seven-fold, Łódź trebled theirs, London and Donostia – San Sebastián both gave double. As the money was not flowing from external sources, our own forces had to be mobilised. Although, without the Goethe-Institut, which also gave more money, and the reduction of the project team's fees it would not have worked. I think it was worth doing.

SH: I agree with Ilina, that the scenarios were enormously important: first to establish relationships and build trust, and second to keep in view the possible approaches to the exhibitions in the different locations. Suddenly, one could get a picture of the possible exhibitions, and I think this is what finally persuaded all those taking part.

IK: We were convinced by the project from the very beginning. However, we had to take a great hurdle with the application for the European Union, or, to put it differently, with "the high art of bureaucracy".

BS: Clearly, there are huge barriers associated with it. I wonder how many institutions can actually master an EU proposal? One needs a secure institutional infrastructure and professionals who are familiar with the process, and, without doubt, certain institutions do not have these opportunities or capacities. Ultimately, finding a solution for those, which have difficulties acquiring funding, has been important for our project, too.

IK: EU applications are a mirror on what is achievable in Europe. So, on

Barbara Steiner, Ilina Koralova, Sabine Hentzsch

the one hand there is a huge effort to support culture, but on the other hand the bureaucratic endeavours associated with it scares many people off. If one knows about the procedures and rules, then some things are less complicated. Some, such as this automated processing system, are of great help for instance. The applicants do not have to create their own spreadsheets anymore and the ones provided are really well thought through. In short: the application has a compelling logic, but it is not always easily accessible.

SH: That is absolutely right. One should not forget that it was not created to torment people, but it upholds the regulations of a large authority, which is required to make its funding transparent and open to justification at any time. This doesn't lend itself to simple procedures. Sure, there are not just the EU rules, one also has to pay attention to the terms and regulations of third-party funding – and the more participants there are, the more difficult this is. The Goethe-Institut is not without its red tape either, but the main reason for this is that it deals with taxpayers' money, which requires accurateness.

BS: The case is different with private funding, but this does not mean it is necessarily easier. Private institutions are a bit more liberal in terms of regulations. However, one can hear "we cannot support a conference in Macau, because it is not relevant for us, why not in Beijing or Shanghai?" Highest public visibility, which is equal to public attention, was expected all the way along the line. To put it differently: there are certain places that are socially and politically off the map of attention or funding. But, as always, there are positive exceptions: The Robert Bosch Foundation backs precisely those places that are not located at the centre of public attention. I am really happy that they supported the projects in Novi Sad and Minsk.

IK: Is it not ironic that it was in these places our project has been enthusiastically reported about. I am thinking about the project in Minsk, which has triggered intense discussion in the unofficial art scene and was publicised and discussed an unbelievable much online. In other cities, like London, there has almost been nothing.

BS: Well, in Germany the project was completely ignored, too, although it was initiated by the German institution Goethe-Institut, and started with a festival at the Haus der Kulturen der Welt.

SH: It is difficult to get the work we do abroad into the German press. This is something we have experienced before. With this project it is even harder, because it is made up of so many locations. There is not one singular location that one can focus on. This is why it was so important to have the opening festival for *Europe (to the power of) n* in Berlin. Nevertheless, the project remains still intangible for many. Actually, we came to the festival with our ideas, our concepts. It was before the projects at the various locations started.

IK: At that time it was impossible to say anything definitive about the individual sites. Therefore, we could offer nothing more than concepts. Basically, this was the reason for including films and performances in the festival programme as tangible time-based artistic formats. However, people were expecting *one* exhibition about Europe and *one* curator. Decentralisation is definitely a hurdle for the promotion of the project.

BS: During a conversation with Markus Müller, who was responsible for Press and Public Relations, he gave me interesting reasons as to why the entire project *Europe (to the power of) n* had such a small media response: first, most people are sick of the subject Europe, it is omnipresent; second, curiosity for places like Minsk, Novi Sad, or Łódź is not very pronounced. Most of all, people from the art sector think that nothing great is happening in these places. In addition, we were facing the problem that *Europe (to the power of) n* cannot be translated into a simple narrative – it is too complex, it cannot be reduced to the single persona – there is no super-curator or super-artist and no overall outlook. In short, the project challenges all the key triggers necessary for successful public relations.

IK: I guess this is the reason there were many more reports about the single exhibitions and projects in specific places. They had what the overall project did not provide: one place, one curator, one concept, one catalogue, whereas *Europe (to the power of) n* multiplies all these factors.

BS: What we are talking about here is basically the consequence of the conception of *Europe (to the power of) n*, which was also conceived as an attempt to challenge expectations of large-scale projects. It questions simple narratives and it deliberately complicates debates about Europe. Certainly, this makes it more difficult for media coverage, but it supports a model of Europe, which takes complexity as a point of departure and is not afraid of keeping it as a stimulating force.

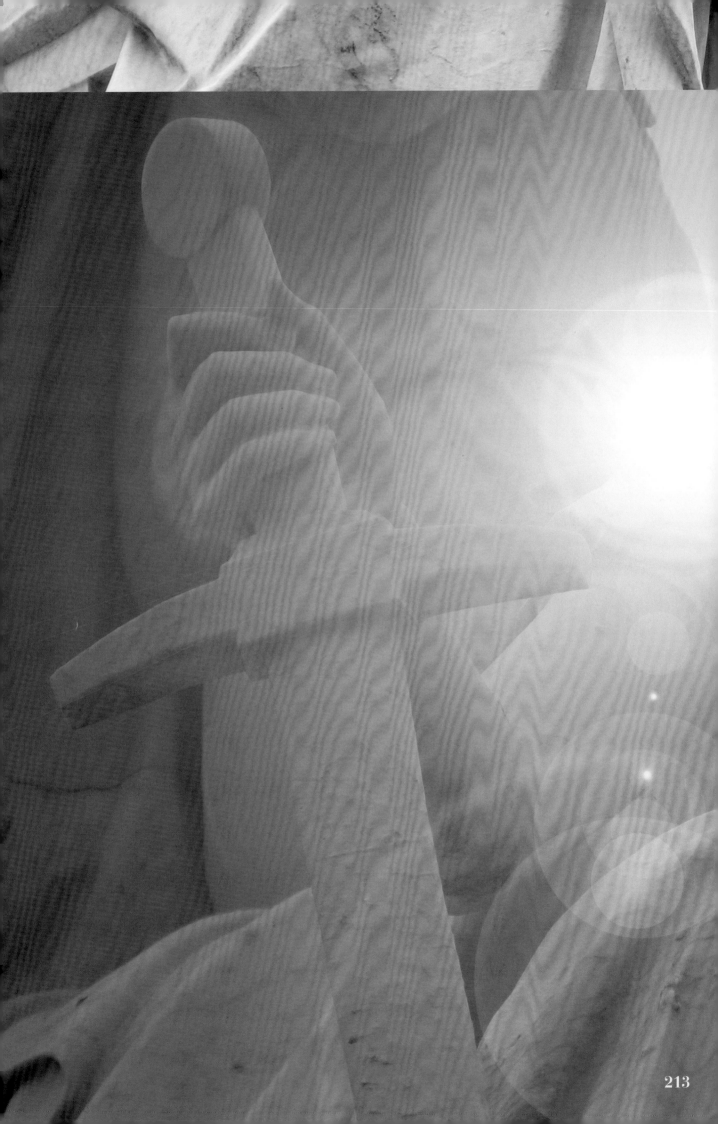

ICH-WILL-EUROPA.DE

ICH-WILL-EUROPA.DE

ICH-WILL-EUROPA.DE

Campaign by The Engaged Europeans,
I want Europe – Philipp Lahm / Presley Antoine / Bettina Zimmermann, 2012
(film stills)

The Making of Europe

Barbara Steiner

The initiative for the project started in 2008. Sabine Hentzsch, at that time director of the Goethe-Institut in Bucharest, and Heiko Sievers, at that time director of the Goethe-Institut in Alexandria, invited Barbara Steiner, at that time director of the Museum for Contemporary Art in Leipzig, to conceive an exhibition about Europe that takes place at five to eight venues in and outside Europe. In the following two years, Steiner travelled to potential locations, talked to potential partner institutions and curators,[1] and finally assembled a project team, which consisted of curators, designers, architects, and a programmer with various backgrounds – as far as training and experience are concerned – and who come from different generations and cultural contexts. These profiles guaranteed a multiplicity of thoughts and approaches that seemed to be appropriate for a reflection about "Europe", which is manifold itself.

However, collaborative projects require time to be developed. Therefore, the start of the project, initially planned for 2010, was very soon dismissed and set up for 2011. The project was divided into two consecutive parts: *Scenarios about Europe* allowed speculation, reflection, and the continuous reformulation of thoughts about Europe, whereas *Europe (to the power of) n* focused on the concrete implementation of artistic projects at the various locations. Due to the involvement of institutions of various sizes and types, along with a large number of contributors, the complexity of the project was already becoming evident at the planning stage.[2] As a consequence, *Scenarios about Europe* formed the testing ground for how to approach a highly complex topic such as Europe through contemporary art, and how a collaborative project with this objective could be initiated at all. The study was done in collaboration with the Museum of Contemporary Art in Leipzig. The extended time frame had become particularly important for the project development, because most funding structures do not apply to long-term projects and multiple partnerships with an uncertain outcome. Generally speaking, carrying out such large projects requires a detailed working plan beforehand. However, collaborative projects, which branch out and change according to various inputs from the partners involved, and which are built on growing mutual trust, make it difficult to define results in advance. Seen against this setting, the Goethe-Institut's readiness to go for a preparatory period allowed gaining all details necessary for the extensive funding procedures that made the actual implementation at various locations in and outside Europe possible.[3] The organiser of *Europe (to the power of) n* was the Goethe-Institut in London.

1 The planned collaborations with Athens and Alexandria could not be realised. For various reasons, the institutions did not want to participate in such a large project. For each location, one curator and one institution were invited. The curator did not necessarily have to be an employee of the institution.

2 A first meeting of potential participants took place in Munich in June 2010, followed by another one in February 2011 in Leipzig. The aim was to sound out the possibilities for establishing a project group, which agreed in carrying out a long-term project.

3 Besides the Goethe-Institut, the preparatory phase was supported by the Cultural Foundation of the Free State of Saxony and the Allianz Cultural Foundation. *Europe (to the power of) n* was backed by the Goethe-Institut, the Robert Bosch Foundation, the Cultural Programme of the European Union, Arend Oetker, Berlin, and the co-organisers: the Curating Contemporary Art Programme, Royal College of Art, London; the Muzeum Sztuki, Łódź; the Henie-Onstad Kunstsenter, Høvikodden near Oslo; and the Office for European Capital of Culture 2016 in Donostia – San Sebastián.

(to the power of) n

Whereas *Scenarios about Europe* was a common project with the same conditions for everyone, *Europe (to the power of) n* brought the differences between the various locations and local conditions into the foreground. Again, the budget available was separated into equal parts. However, the purchasing power of one and the same amount differed in the respective countries. In wealthier countries, 30,000 Euro – this was the amount everyone got from the overall budget – are mostly inadequate for doing an ambitious art project, in less wealthy ones it guarantees a great amount of leeway. This obvious disadvantage of some corresponds with their advantage when it comes to the general funding of art projects. Many sources of financial support are available in Norway, United Kingdom, and Belgium, in spite of the high level of competition in these countries. On the other hand, there is little (and if so, it is mostly from private sources) or no funding for contemporary art in Serbia, Turkey, Belarus, or China; often, promotional authorities do not even exist. *Europe (to the power of) n* started under the premise of equality: each curator/institution should get the same status in the project development and the same amount from the overall budget, and each one should be subjected to the same obligations for the joint agendas.[4] Employing the principle of equality intended, in paradoxical reversal, to reveal and make aware of inequality and given asymmetries the project partners had to deal with and, in fact, dealt with.[5]

However, when it came to the realisation of the project, the radical implementation of equality seemed to be impossible. The funding rules that the Cultural Programme of the European Union provides distinguish between organiser, co-organisers, and associated partners. An important difference in this allocation is, for example, the administration of the grant: whereas the co-organisers administer their budget themselves and have to contribute to the general budget, the associated partners do not have to contribute financially. As a consequence, the organiser has to manage the associated partners's expenses.[6] Nevertheless, in *Europe (to the power of) n* equality was kept in regard of the general resources available to all participants and in the conceptualisation of the project, but was given up in its administration. To make the planned projects happen for the associated partners in Minsk, Novi Sad, İstanbul, and Beijing/Taipei, the organiser took administrative and legal responsibility, but left the conceptual elaboration and the practical realisation on-site entirely up to the curators.

After setting the frame for the project, the details of carrying out projects such as *Europe (to the power of) n* showed the usual managerial difficulties of collaborations under such a wide range of conditions. In the political sector, restrictions did not occur during the entire course

4   There was only one small difference in the obligations for the joint agendas: three of four common conferences were held at the co-organisers's institutions, because they were able to provide the infrastructure necessary for hosting the conferences. The fourth co-organiser, the Office for European Capital of Culture 2016, Donostia – San Sebastián, joined later, after the first application to the Cultural Programme of the European Union was made.

5   The curator for Novi Sad developed his exhibition around political, economic, cultural, and social asymmetries, which was also expressed in the title *Asymmetric Europe.*

6   Not all partners were able to contribute financially due to a lack of resources. The contributions of the co-organisers went into their own projects. They were able to significantly raise their budgets. In the case of Norway, the final project budget was more than three times higher than the amount coming from the overall budget of *Europe (to the power of) n.*

of the project as might have been expected in countries such as Belarus or China. Although the exhibition in Minsk was done shortly before the presidential election and after the extradition of the Swedish ambassador, and some artworks were openly critical[7], there was no censorship from the authorities – even though concerns had been voiced in preparation of the project there. The project took place at the "private, commercial" Gallery Ў. Obviously, it is the private sector, which offers space to contemporary art activities. Although not directly comparable, in this regard the foundation of Vitamin Creative Space was driven by a similar agenda. When it was founded in Guangzhou and later in Beijing, it responded to both financial necessities and limited possibilities of art institutions in the People's Republic of China.[8] Again, the private sector has provided opportunities for the contemporary art scenes the state sector would not allow. With the invitation of Taiwan, the Taipei Contemporary Art Center was chosen. The TCAC was responsible for the print-on-demand publication of the Chinese part of *Europe (to the power of) n* and its short version published in the *Artco Monthly Magazine*, participated in the Beijing conference, and presented the outcome of the project in Taipei. Its assigned role was that of a critical "satellite" orbiting the project and having a share in it.

In the economic sector, some difficulties seemed to be almost banal at first sight, but on closer inspection bordered on existential issues, at least for those concerned. International payment transactions to Serbia, Belarus, Turkey, and China are not only very extensive and labourious, but also the bank charges are high in comparison to the very often low fees.[9] This means that in countries where, for example, fees are generally low, disadvantages in the payment procedures are faced.[10] In addition to this, not everybody involved in *Europe (to the power of) n* had a bank account. And quite often cash payments are still very common in the field of commerce in Turkey and China. However, when it comes to the conditions determined by funding institutions, cash payments are supposed to be an exception.[11] Concluding here, it must be said that mechanisms of inclusion and exclusion are already manifested in the parameters of carrying out cultural projects. This is exactly why *Europe (to the power of) n* is not only concerned with artistic ideas about Europe, but also with the regulatory framework, the contexts, and the conditions that make collaborative projects possible or impossible.

7   The critical remarks addressed, for example, the heroising of the glorious Belarusian past, or caricatured Alexander Lukashenko's failed accreditation to the Olympic Games in London.

8   The People's Republic of China does not allow independent foundations or private art associations.

9   Only two countries involved in the project, Belgium and Spain, participate in the European currency union. All others operate with national currencies, and only two of them – the EU-members United Kingdom and Poland – are entitled to simplifications in international payment transactions.

10 Within *Europe (to the power of) n,* the bank charges were considered in the project's budget and not distracted from the service/fee paid for.

11 Some organisations, such as the Robert Bosch Foundation, which have conducted projects in many of these countries involved in *Europe (to the power of) n* and know about the difficulties, accept cash payments.

Following pages:
FLORIAN GÖTHNER
Neighbours, 2012
(film stills)

The title of the Europe project is based on two notations: in the headlines and captions $Europe^n$ is used and in the texts, to support a better reading flow, *Europe (to the power of) n.*

BIOGRAPHIES OF PARTICIPANTS

KONRAD ABICHT
studied Computer Sciences at Leipzig University with his main focus on software development and semantic web as well as on theoretical aspects of computer sciences, such as the organisation of information. He earned his Bachelor's degree in Computer Science in 2011 and his Master's degree in 2013, both at Leipzig University. Since 2010, he has worked in several projects in the fields of culture, art and design mediation, information design, and information architecture research.

PEIO AGUIRRE
is a writer, art critic, independent curator, and editor based in Donostia – San Sebastián, Basque Country, Spain. Since the late 1990s he has been organising art projects in the Basque context, connecting local practices with the international art scene. Until 2005, he was co-director of the curatorial platform D.A.E. Donostiako Arte Ekinbideak, an independent agency for the development of ephemeral publishing as well as art projects related to public space. As a writer, he is interested in subjects such as modernism, Marxism, form and formalism, and also science fiction. In his critical approach, he pursues an explicit interest in the local context and how this is penetrated by global developments. His projects and curated exhibitions include: *The Great Method*, Casco Office for Art, Design and Theory, Utrecht, 2007; *Images from the Other Side*, CAAM, Canary Island, 2007; *Archaelogies of the Future*, sala rekalde, Bilbao, 2007; *Asier Mendizabal*, MACBA, Museum for Contemporary Art, Barcelona, 2008; *Nestor Basterretxea: Form and Universe*, Bilbao Fine Arts Museum, 2013; *Apolonija Sustersic*, *Auditorium / Display,* MUSAC, León, 2013.

CHRISTINE BOCK
is a Master's Student in Urban Design at the Institute of Technology in Berlin. In 2010, she graduated with a Bachelor of Arts degree in Spatial Strategies / Interior Design at the Muthesius Academy of Fine Arts and Design in Kiel. She has contributed to several projects by Raumlabor Berlin on the subject of artistic interventions in public spaces, exploring cities in transformation as well as the borders between public and private sphere. In collaboration with Christian Teckert, she has developed concepts on exhibition design since 2012. Christine Bock is interested in research, analysis, and intervention in public space and its daily practices.

LARA FRESKO
is a writer, researcher, and cultural worker based in İstanbul. She has an MA in Comparative Literature from İstanbul Bilgi University and a BA in Cultural Studies from Sabancı University, İstanbul. Her research interests include printed matter, archival work, and collective and collaborative structures.

KIT HAMMONDS
is a curator based in London. His work encompasses exhibition making, events, education, and writing, focusing on collaborative production, be it in social, community, or "third-sector" groups; or under institutional, corporate, or political structures. Currently, he is the Second Year Lead Tutor on the Curating MA at the Royal College of Art, where he works with students on their collectively curated projects. He is co-founder of Publish and be Damned, a voluntary organisation focused on artist-led publishing, a project he continues to run. Previously, he was curator at the South London Gallery, where among his group exhibitions he staged a series that recast the gallery as a playground, *Games & Theory;* a nightclub, *The Weasel,* and an afro-futurist commune, *The Mothership Collective.*

TONE HANSEN
is director of Henie-Onstad Kunstsenter. Her recent exhibitions and projects include: *Learning for Life* in collaboration with Ane Hjort Guttu, *Modernism Machine,* and the reader *Entering a Site of Production* in collaboration with Dag Erik Elgin and the Academy of Art, Oslo, both in 2012. Her 2011 exhibitions include: *In Translation* with Saskia Holmkvist, *World Rehearsal Court* with Judy Radul, as well as the reader and symposium *A Thousand Eyes: Media technology, the law and the aesthetics. The Creative Act* and the retrospective presentation of *Hito Steyerl* took place in 2010 and *To be Heard is to be Seen* in 2009. Hansen is the editor of the newly published reader *(Re)Staging the Art Museum* with Revolver Publishing. She held a research position at the Oslo National Academy of Art in Oslo from 2003 until 2008. She was acting chairman of Young Artists Society from 2003 until 2005. Other projects include the 2007 exhibition and publication *Megamonstermuseum. How to Imagine a Museum of Today?* as well as the anthologies *The New Administration of Aesthetics* and *What Does Public Mean? Art as a Participant in the Public Arena,* both published in 2007.

OLIVER KLIMPEL
is a designer and runs the studio Büro International London. After gaining a Diploma at the Academy of Visual Arts Leipzig and a Masters degree at the Royal College of Art London he was appointed Professor for System-Design at the Leipzig Art Academy in 2008. In this capacity, he combines alternative and experimental forms of educational situations with research-based forms of design. He writes frequently about art, design, and visual

culture and works on design projects – amongst them publications, visual identities, and exhibition designs for numerous institutions, e. g. Tate Modern and Tate Britain. Recent projects include book designs in collaboration with artists, an architectural design for an apartment block in Dortmund, and an exhibition about his educational work at the Brandenburgischer Kunstverein Potsdam.

CHRISTOPHER KÖHLER
graduated in Cultural Studies, Communication and Media Science, and American Studies from the University of Leipzig in 2011. Shortly afterwards, he entered *Scenarios about Europe* as project assistant, editor, and translator continuing this work within the *Europe (to the power of) n* project. Furthermore, he has been part of the Europe^n online development team. Köhler is a PhD student at the American Studies Institute at Leipzig University. His main areas of research are modern mythology and consumer culture in the US. Köhler works as a freelance translator and editor in Leipzig.

ILINA KORALOVA
works as freelance curator based in Leipzig. Between 2002 and 2009, she worked as a curator at the Museum of Contemporary Art Leipzig (GfZK). Since 2007, she has been a lecturer at the Faculty for Cultural Studies at the University of Leipzig. Her subject is the structural organisation and funding strategies of cultural institutions, as well as the practical aspects of curating exhibitions. Within the framework of various research and exhibition projects, she has curated several group and solo exhibitions dealing mainly with the heritage of socialist modernism, post-socialist urban conditions, and social tolerance. Koralova studied Art History at the Academy of Fine Arts in Sofia.

JAROSŁAW LUBIAK
is a curator at Muzeum Sztuki in Łódź and lecturer at the Art Academy of Szczecin. He graduated from the Institute of Art History at the Adam Mickiewicz University in Poznań and from the School of Social Sciences at the Polish Academy of Sciences, Institute of Philosophy and Sociology in Warsaw, where he earned his PhD in 2009. He is interested in the transformations of contemporary art and the history of 20th-century art in relation to contemporary philosophy and socio-political and economic changes, particularly the transformation of the public sphere. Among others, Lubiak has curated the following exhibitions: *Correspondences. Modern Art and Universalism* (with Małgorzata Ludwisiak), Muzeum Sztuki, Łódź, 2012–2013; *Afterimages of life. Władysław Strzemiński and Rights for Art* (with Paulina Kurc-Maj), Muzeum Sztuki, Łódź, 2010–2011; *The Parallax and the Gaze of Zbigniew Rogalski*,

Muzeum Sztuki, Łódź, 2010–2011; *Hostipitality. Receiving Strangers* (with Kamil Kuskowski), Muzeum Sztuki, Łódź, 2010. He is the author of numerous essays and critical texts as well as editor of publications, for example: *Katja Strunz. Zeittraum #9 für Władysław Strzemiński*, Muzeum Sztuki, Łódź / Walther König, Köln 2011; *Museum as a Luminous Object of Desire*, Muzeum Sztuki, Łódź, 2010.

FILIP LUYCKX
graduated in Modern History from the University Leuven. Since 1994, he has been responsible for the exhibition and publication programme at Sint-Lukas Art Foundation in Brussels, where he has delivered an innovative programme of contemporary artists from both Belgium and abroad – among them Richard Billingham, Jan De Cock, Nathalie Djurberg, Rainer Ganahl, Rodney Graham, Frank Nitsche, Yehudit Sasportas, Nedko Solakov, and Anne-Mie Van Kerckhoven. He has also curated large-scale museum exhibitions, for example *Critical Elegance* at the Museum Dhondt-Dhaenens, Deurle; *Dream Extensions* at SMAK, Gent; and *Ephemeral Fringes* at Art Brussels. He has edited a number of publications including the collection catalogues for *Frac du Nord–Pas de Calais, Honoré d'O* at Frac Champagne-Ardenne Reims, *Frank Nitsche* at Haus am Waldsee Berlin, and *Lori Hersberger* at Kunstmuseum Basel.

LENA PRENTS
is an independent art historian and curator. After studying German Philology at the Linguistic University in Minsk and Art History and German Literature at the Free University of Berlin, she worked for the German Guggenheim Berlin, the Bauhaus Museum Weimar, and the Museum for Contemporary Art Leipzig. Her work focuses on the interrelation of art and exhibition practice in connection with socio-political discourses. She is currently working on her PhD dissertation on socialist modernist architecture in contemporary art. Since 2006, Lena Prents has been teaching at the European Humanities University in Vilnius, a Belarusian university in exile. She lives in Berlin.

ESRA SARIGEDIK ÖKTEM
has been the Head of Arts at the British Council, Turkey, since 2011. Between 2005 and 2007, she worked as a research curator at the Van Abbemuseum, Eindhoven. From 2004 until 2005, she was assistant curator for the 9th International İstanbul Biennial. Between 2008 and 2011, Sarigedik Öktem run a the project initiated by the British Council titled *My City,* a large-scale art in the public realm project realised in different cities in Turkey. In this connection, commissioned works by artists from across Europe, and a residency programme in several European art institutions for artists from

Turkey were realised. Esra Sarigedik Öktem's lectures and texts are centred around nationalism and contemporary art.

TRISTAN SCHULZE
studied Computer Sciences and Japanese Studies at the University of Leipzig and later Interface Design at the University of Applied Sciences in Dessau. He graduated with diploma in the field of interaction and information design in 2009. Since 2010, Schulze has worked as an interaction and interface designer. He teaches around this subject at the FH Magdeburg, FH Dessau, and HFK Bremen. As a member of the artistic collective Team Hello, he established Hello Studios, an independent studio project in 2006.

JOANNA SOKOŁOWSKA
is an art historian and curator working at the Muzeum Sztuki in Łódź. She is interested in the politics of art in relation to labour, economy, governance, and historical narratives. Her curatorial projects include the following, among others: *Untimely Stories* (with Jarosław Lubiak), Muzeum Sztuki, Łódź, 2012; *Eyes Looking for a Head to Inhabit* (with Aleksandra Jach, Katarzyna Słoboda, Magdalena Ziółkowska), Muzeum Sztuki, Łódź, 2011; *Workers Leaving the Workplace*, Muzeum Sztuki, Łódź, 2010; *Accretions* (with Angela Harutyunyan, Tevž Logar), Galerija Škuc, Ljubljana, 2010; *Another City, Another Life* (with Benjamin Cope), Zachęta National Gallery of Art, Warsaw, 2009.

BARBARA STEINER
is a curator and writer. Currently, she is the Artistic Director of *Europe (to the power of) n*, which takes place at eleven venues in and outside the European Union. From 2001 until 2010, she was director of the Museum of Contemporary Art Leipzig (GfZK). Steiner's interest focuses on politics of representation, architecture, and display. In her projects, she takes political, economic, social, and cultural conditions of artistic and curatorial work as a conceptual starting point and draws particular interest to various (sometimes rivalling) concerns, constraints, and the respective interconnected processes of negotiation. Steiner studied Art History and Political Science at the University of Vienna. She wrote her doctoral thesis on the Ideology of the White Cube. Together with as-if berlinwien, Steiner published *Negotiating Spaces,* 2010. In the same year *The Captured Museum* was brought out, followed by *Scenarios about Europe* in 2012. In summer 2013 *Superkilen* will be issued in collaboration with the Bjarke Ingels Group, Topotek1, and Superflex.

MIŠKO ŠUVAKOVIĆ
teaches Aesthetics and Theory of Art at the Faculty of Music in Belgrade as well as Theory of Art and Theory of Culture for

the Interdisciplinary Postgraduate Studies Programme at the University of Art Belgrade. His theoretical work has been focused on the study of contemporary art, culture and education. His artistic and theoretical research started in the tradition of Wittgenstein's philosophy of language in the early seventies. Later, he explored discursive practices of the neo-avant-garde and contemporary visual art, contemporary performing arts and curatorial-political practice. He is interested in self-organised artistic and theoretical education.

CHRISTIAN TECKERT
is a Professor for Space / Concept at the Muthesius Academy of Fine Arts and Design in Kiel, and a lecturer at the Institute of Art and Architecture at the Academy of Fine Arts Vienna. Together with Andreas Spiegl, he founded the Office for Cognitive Urbanism in 1999. Several projects have evolved in this context, such as *Studiocity* at the IPZ Vienna / Kunstverein Wolfsburg in 1999, *Screenclimbing* at the Kunstverein in Hamburg in 2000, *Last Minute* at the GfZK Leipzig in 2006, and *ManifeSTATION* for the Manifesta7 – Rovereto in 2008. In 2001, together with Paul Grundei and Stephanie Kaindl, he founded the architectural office as-if berlinwien, which realised the new exhibition building for the GfZK Leipzig in 2005. Teckert writes and publishes regularly on the subject of the intersection of art, architecture, spatial theory, and urbanism. He is co-author and co-editor of the publications *Prospekt*, and *Last Minute*, both published by Walther König, Cologne, as well as *Negotiating Spaces*, published by Jovis, Berlin. Together with Andreas Fogarasi, he is the curator and designer of the exhibition *Eastern Promises* at the MAK Vienna, 2013, publication forthcoming by Hatje Cantz.

FLORIAN WÜST
is an artist and independent film curator living in Berlin whose work revolves around the history of post-war Germany and modern technical progress. He studied Fine Arts at the Braunschweig School of Art and received his master's degree from the Piet Zwart Institute, Rotterdam. Recent curatorial projects include: *Becoming Voice*, South London Gallery, London, 2012 (with Maxa Zoller); *White Noise*, Irish Film Institute, Dublin, 2012; *Jailbreak*, Impakt Festival, Utrecht, 2011; Über Lebenskunst Festival, Haus der Kulturen der Welt, Berlin, 2011; *Crashing Markets*, 25 FPS International Festival of Experimental Film and Video, Zagreb, 2010; *Berlin am Kabel*, Kino Arsenal, Berlin, 2010. Wüst frequently writes and lectures about topics related to film and society. Together with Stefanie Schulte Strathaus, he is editor of *Who says concrete doesn't burn, have you tried? West Berlin Film in the '80s*, 2008.

JUN YANG
lives and works in Taipei, Vienna, and Yokohama. He studied at the Gerrit Rietveld Academy in Amsterdam and at the Academy of Fine Arts, Vienna. Having grown up in various cultural contexts, in his artistic work Yang investigates the influence of media images on concepts of identity. Together with other curators and artists, he was responsible for the foundation of the Taipei Contemporary Art Center. As an artist, Jun Yang has participated in Manifesta 4, 2002; Venice Biennial, 2005; Taipei Biennial, 2008; and Gwangju Biennial, 2012. He is represented by: Martin Janda Gallery, Vienna; Vitamin Creative Space, Guangzhou, Beijing; and ShugoArts, Tokyo.

GOETHE-INSTITUT DIRECTORS

FRANK BAUMANN
Director of the Goethe-Institut in Minsk since 2011. Previously, he worked as librarian at the Goethe-Institut in Moscow.

GEORG BLOCHMANN
Director of the Goethe-Institut in Warsaw. Previously, he was Director of the Goethe-Institut in Tel Aviv and Head of Programme South-East Europe in Athens.

JOHANNES EBERT
General Secretary of the Goethe-Institut since 2012. Previously, he was Head of the Goethe-Institut and the region of Eastern Europe / Central Asia in Moscow and Head of the Goethe-Institut and the region North Africa / Middle East in Cairo.

BERTHOLD FRANKE
Director of the Goethe-Institut in Brussels, Regional Director for South-West Europe and Commissioner for the European Union since 2009. He was formerly Regional Director for South-West Europe in Paris.

CLAUDIA HAHN-RAABE
Director of the Goethe-Institut in İstanbul. She has also worked in Brussels, New York, Boston, and in the Headquarter in Munich.

MARGARETA HAUSCHILD
Director of the Goethe-Institut in Madrid since 2009. Formerly, she was Director of the Goethe-Institut in Brussels and Commissioner for the European Union.

SABINE HENTZSCH
Director of the Goethe-Institut in London and Regional Director for North-West Europe. She was previously Director of the Goethe-Institut in Bucharest, Romania.

JOHANNA M. KELLER
Director of the Goethe-Institut in Vilnius since 2010. She worked previously at the Goethe-Institut in Damascus.

MATTHIAS MÜLLER-WIEFERIG
Director of the Goethe-Institut Belgrade and former he was Director of the Goethe-Institut in Copenhagen.

KRISTIANE ZAPPEL
Director of the Goethe-Institut in Oslo since 2010. Prior to this, she was Director of the Goethe-Institut in Bogotá, Colombia.

PICTURE CREDITS

LIST OF WORKS

NEIGHBOURS

pp. 38–39, 40–41, 42

LONDON

p. 27
Slavs and Tatars
Triangulation (Not Moscow, Not Mecca)
2012
Concrete, paint; $27 \times 24 \times 23$ cm
Courtesy of Kraup-Tuskany Zeider, Berlin

pp. 28, 30, 33
Hannes Zebedin
What's Happening Tottenham?
2012
Various materials; Approx. $750 \times 230 \times 120$ cm
Courtesy of the artist

p.28
detail:
Hannes Zebedin
Blind But Awake (Coincidental Harmony Monument #1)
2012
2 espresso cups, coffee, contact lenses, hand-written text; Dimensions variable
Courtesy of the artist

p. 29
Daniel James Wilkinson
The Thellusionists
2012
Mixed media installation; Dimensions variable
Courtesy of the artist

p. 31
Marisol Malatesta
Tildados de Mondernos
2011
Pencil on found paper; 25×38 cm
Courtesy of the artist

Marisol Malatesta
Calvary from Right to Left
2011
Pencil on found paper; 25×38 cm
Courtesy of the artist

Marisol Malatesta
M.-.R.-.H.-.
2012
Pencil on found paper; 45×60 cm
Courtesy of the artist

p. 33–34
Nils Norman
Romney Reborn
1996–2012
Inkjet on Somerset photo paper; 90×150 cm
Courtesy of the artist

Nils Norman
The Commune of Lydd
2012
Inkjet on Somerset photo paper; 90×150 cm
Courtesy of the artist

Nils Norman
The Jury's Gap Phalanstery
2012
Inkjet on Somerset photo paper; 90×150 cm
Courtesy of the artist

p. 34
Marisol Malatesta
Tolerencia no. 18
2012
Pencil on found paper; 45×60 cm
Courtesy of the artist

Marisol Malatesta
Under the Influence
2012
Pencil on found paper; 45×60 cm
Courtesy of the artist

Marisol Malatesta
Three Way Progression
2012
Pencil on found paper; 38×25 cm
Courtesy of the artist

Marisol Malatesta
From the Last Landowner
2012
Pencil on found paper; 25×38 cm
Courtesy of the artist

Marisol Malatesta
Design, Calculation and Optimisation
2012
Pencil on found paper; 25×38 cm
Courtesy of the artist

MINSK

p. 46
Sergey Shabohin
We Are Stern Consumers of Cultural Revolutions
2012
Various materials; Various sizes
Courtesy of the artist

pp. 45, 47, 49, 94
Michaël Aerts
Mobile Monument Performance
2009 / 2012
Existing out of mobile monuments and performance by different social groups in Minsk; Dimensions variable
Courtesy of DEWEER GALLERY, Belgium

pp. 48, 96
Goldin+Senneby (with Swedish County Administrative Boards)
Not Approved: Field Inspection Photographs of Rejected Landscape Features
2009–2011
32 c-prints; Various sizes
Courtesy of the artists

p. 49
Andrei Liankevich
Double Heroes
2012
C-print; 150×100 cm
Courtesy of the artist

pp. 50–51
Jura Shust
London
2012
Dispersion paint on wall; 540×100 cm
Courtesy of the artist

pp. 52–53
Marina Naprushkina
Wealth for All
2011
Video, 10 min
Courtesy of the artist

p. 56
After Effect
2012
Poster, design by Hleb Makeyeu
Courtesy of the designer and
European Humanities University

Reclaiming the City
2012
Poster, design by Hleb Makeyeu
Courtesy of the designer and
European Humanities University

ŁÓDŹ

p. 59
Anikó Loránt – Kaszás Tamás (ex-artists
collective)
Famine Food
Since 2011
Mixed media materials (drawings, prints, texts,
photos, digital screens, and objects), installed
on wood construction; Dimensions variable
Courtesy of the artists

p. 60
Gast Bouschet & Nadine Hilbert
A Planet (Svínafellsjökull, Iceland)
June 2011–June 2012
6 photographies on photographic canvas,
89 × 133 cm
Courtesy of the artists

pp. 60–61
Anikó Loránt – Kaszás Tamás (ex-artists
collective)
Famine Food
Since 2011
Mixed media materials (drawings, prints, texts,
photos, digital screens and objects), installed on
wood construction; Dimensions variable
Courtesy of the artists

p. 63
Slavs and Tatars
Reverse Joy
2012
Public intervention in Łódź
Courtesy of the artists

p. 64
Wendelien van Oldenborgh
Supposing I Love You and You Also Love Me
2011
Architectural setting with bench and projec-
tion (montage of still frame with text, sound,
English and Polish subtitles), 13 min
Courtesy of Wilfried Lentz Gallery in Rotterdam
and the artist

pp. 64–65
Nástio Mosquito
3 Continents (Europa, America, Africa)
2010
Video installation, 7 min 40 s
Courtesy of the artist

pp. 64–65, 93
Aleksander Komarov
Palipaduazennije (Паліпадуацэннé)
(part of the project Language Lesson)
2011
DVD, 21 min
Courtesy of the artist

p. 65
Peter Friedl
Theory of Justice
2008
Photograph series; Various sizes
Courtesy of Galerie Meyer Kainer

pp. 66–67
Ahmet Öğüt
Mutual Issues, Inventive Acts
2008
A series of photographs; Each 150 × 100 cm,
charcoal drawings on paper; 18.5 × 25 cm, clo-
thes hangers, light bulbs, a table; Dimensions
variable
Courtesy of the artist

p. 68
Jérémie Boyard
On the Verge of a Down
2010
Destroyed and cut up police barrier;
115 × 100 × 40 cm
Courtesy of the artist

İSTANBUL

pp. 81–85
Banu Cennetoğlu
The List
2012
Various materials; Various sizes
Open source material,
www.unitedagainstracism.org

pp. 86–87
Isaac Julien
Frantz Fanon: Black Skin White Mask I
1996
DVD, 52 min (film still)
Courtesy of the artist and Victoria Miro Gallery,
London

p. 88
Isaac Julien
Cast No Shadow (Western Union Series No.1)
2007
Duratrans Image in Lightbox; 120 × 120 cm
Courtesy of the artist and Victoria Miro Gallery,
London

EXCHANGE

p. 92
Sketch by Artistic Director Barbara Steiner

Nils Norman
Updated Social Composition of Romney Marsh
2011/12
Inkjet on Somerset photo paper
Courtesy of the artist

p. 95
Asako Iwama
Incorporation
2012
Artist: Asako Iwama, Actor: Matthias Neukirch,
Camera: Joji Koyama and Montse Torreda

p. 97
Slavs and Tatars
Reverse Joy
2012
Installation; Dimensions variable
Courtesy of the artist

p. 98
Köken Ergun
Binibining Promised Land
2009–2010
Video, 30 min (film still)
Courtesy of the artist

p. 99
Jun Yang
Paris Syndrome
2007–2008
Video, 10 min (film still)
Courtesy of Galerie Martin Janda, Wien

HØVIKODDEN / OSLO

p. 103
Priscila Fernandes
For a Better World
2012
HD-video, 8.3 min (film still)
Courtesy of the artist

pp. 104–105
Darcy Lange
Studies of Three Birmingham Schools
1976
3 videos

Darcy Lange
Studies of Three Birmingham Schools
1976
C-prints
Courtesy of the artist

pp. 106–107
Servet Koçyiğit
Higher Education
2006
C-print; 280 × 400 cm
Courtesy of the artist

pp. 108
Joost Conijn
Siddieqa, Firdaus, Abdallah, Soelayman,
Moestafa, Hawwa, Dzoel-kifl
2004
Video, 44 min
Courtesy of the artist

pp. 94, 110–111
Ane Hjort Guttu
Freedom Requires Free People
2012
HD-video, 33 min
Courtesy of the artist

p. 112
Erik Løchen
Citizens of Tomorrow: A Film About Oslo's
Public Schools
1950
35 mm film transferred to video, 15 min
Courtesy of the artist

pp. 112–113
Oslo School Museum
Students' work, handwriting
1900
Exercise books, cardboard and miscellaneous
documentation; Various sizes

Peter Tillberg
Will You Be Profitable, Little Friend?
1972
Oil on canvas
Courtesy of the artist

p. 114
Oslo School Museum
Students' work, needlework
1920–1980
Approx. 65 works; Various sizes

NOVI SAD

p. 128
Polona Tratnik with Collaborators
Hair in Vitro
2011
3 monitors, digital print; 500 × 100 cm
Courtesy of the artist
p. 129
IRWIN
Time for a New State. Some Say You Can Find
Happiness There
2012
Billbord, digital print; 600 × 284 cm
Courtesy of the artists

p. 130
Nika Radić
The End
2012
Film projection, digital print; 500 × 100 cm
Courtesy of the artist

p. 131
Tadej Pogačar
P.A.R.A.S.I.T.E. Public Sculpture
1999–2010
2 digital prints; Each 70 × 50 cm
Courtesy of the artist

p. 132
Dragomir Ugren
Untitled (wall installation)
2011
10 pieces, acrylic paint on MDF and gauze;
10 × 2 × 1000 cm
Courtesy of the artist

p. 133
Provisional SALTA Ensemble
Monument (Desire for Democracy)
2012
Mixed media, digital print; 160 × 280 × 100 cm
Courtesy of the artists

Zoran Todorović
The Bride
1998
Digital print and projection; 100 × 500 cm
Courtesy of the artist

p. 134
Zorica Čolić
Face Shifting
2005–2007
Digital print; 70 × 50 cm
Courtesy of the artist

BRUSSELS

p. 137
Enrique Marty
Fall of the Idols
2013
195 sculptures, various materials
Dimensions variable
Courtesy of DEWEER GALLERY, Belgium

pp. 138–139
Reza Aramesh
Action 108
2011
Triptych, silver gelatine print, mounted on
aluminium and archival board, framed in
aluminum and glass;
One central panel 191 × 93 × 5 cm; two side
panels, each 191 × 79 × 8 cm
Courtesy of Leila Heller Gallery, New York

Davide Bertocchi
Le Régime
2009
Plastic straw, black Belgian marble, multicolour
onix, travertine marble, red marble, blue lime-
tone; 40 × 30 × 30 cm
Courtesy of the artist and Jarach Gallery, Venice

Clegg & Guttmann
Board of Directors, Version 2
2007
C-print behind acrylic glass on MDF-frame;
170 × 298 × 6 cm
Courtesy of Galerie Christian Nagel, Cologne /
Berlin

pp. 138–139, 146
Heidi Voet
Stars & Constellations
2012
Coins, tokens
Courtesy of the artist

p. 140
Tony Matelli
Yesterday
2009
Painted bronze; 104 × 35 × 31 cm
Courtesy of Stephane Simoens Contemporary
Fine Art, Knokke

Tim Eitel
Architect
2012
Oil on canvas; 210 × 250 cm
Courtesy of Galerie Eigen & Art Berlin / Leipzig

Helmut Stallaerts
Die Auflösung
2009
C-print on diasec; 140 × 95 cm
Courtesy of Galerie Albert Baronian, Brussels

p. 142
Philip Metten
Untitled, 2011
Polyester, bronze powder, acryl; 91 × 62 × 38 cm
Courtesy of the artist

Sylvie Fleury
A Journey to Fitness or How to Loose
10 Pounds in 3 Weeks
1993–1998
Video installation
Courtesy of the artist

pp. 142–143
Veronica Brovall
Coexist, 2011
Steel, reflectors, screws, break lights, cable,
timer, lights, transparent car lacquer;
116 × 112 × 15 cm
Private collection, Norway

p. 143
Frank Nitsche
EYE-16-2013, 2013
Oil on canvas; 84.5 × 62 cm
Courtesy of Galerie Gebr. Lehmann Berlin /
Dresden

Frank Nitsche
SEM-17-2013, 2013
Oil on canvas; 44 × 49 cm
Courtesy of Galerie Gebr. Lehmann Berlin /
Dresden

Frank Nitsche
WCH-18-2013, 2013
Oil on canvas; 100 × 100 cm
Courtesy of Galerie Gebr. Lehmann Berlin /
Dresden

Frank Nitsche
GIL-19-2013, 2013
Oil on canvas; 89 x 79 cm
Courtesy of Galerie Gebr. Lehmann Berlin /
Dresden

pp. 144–145
Josephine Meckseper
Sanitätshaus Hofman, No 1
2007
C-print; 160 × 233 cm
Courtesy of Galerie Reinhard Hauff, Stuttgart

pp. 146
Koen Vanmechelen
Pedigree – CCP
2013
17 taxidermic chickens, wood; lambda print on
Plexiglas; Dimensions variable
Courtesy of the artist

Nedko Solakov
Political Stories
2012
Sepia, black and white ink, and wash on paper;
series of 12 drawings; each approx. 19 × 28 cm
Courtesy of Galleria Continua, San Gimignano /
Beijing / Le Moulin

p. 147
Ariel Schlesinger
The Kid 2012
2012
Glass, c-print; 114 × 96 cm
Courtesy of Galerie Yvon Lambert Paris

Michaël Aerts
Misala
2009
6 parts, flightcase material, lacquer on wood;
Approx. 80 × 80 × 170 cm
Courtesy of DEWEER GALLERY, Belgium

p. 148
Enrique Marty
Fall of the Idols
2013
195 sculptures, various materials;
Dimensions variable
Courtesy of DEWEER GALLERY, Belgium

232

FILMS

pp. 151, 154–159
Eva Kroll
Europa im Werden – Der Schuman-Plan
1952
16 mm, 10 min (film still)
Courtesy of Kinemathek Hamburg

pp. 152–153
Stuart Legg
The Hour of Choice
1951
35 mm, 20 min (film still)
Courtesy of Deutsches Historisches Museum –
Filmarchiv, Berlin

pp. 160–161
Ernst Niederreither
Wir und die Anderen
1950
16 mm, 14 min (film still)
Courtesy of Bundesarchiv–Filmarchiv, Berlin

SPATIAL IDENTITY

pp. 164–165
Christian Teckert and Christine Bock
The Manual
2012/13
Drawing

pp. 166–167, 168–169
Christian Teckert and Christine Bock
European Exhibition Space
2012/13
Photomontage

DONOSTIA – SAN SEBASTIÁN

p. 173
Asier Mendizabal
Auñamendi
2006–2010
36 colour photographs; Each 30 × 40 cm
Courtesy of the artist

pp. 174, 182–183
Aleksander Komarov
Language Lessons
2012
26 black and white photographs;
Each 30 × 30 cm
Courtesy of the artist

p. 175 (+ p. 98)
Annika Eriksson
Wir Bleiben / The Last Tenants
2011–2013
HD-video, 20 min
Courtesy of the artist

Xabier Salaberria
Unconscious / Conscious
2010
Installation, various materials;
Dimensions variable
Courtesy of the artist

p. 176
Jean-Marie Straub and Danièle Huillet
Europa 2005 – 27 Octobre
2006
Video, 10 min
Courtesy of Straub-Huillet Films

p. 177
Iñaki Garmendia
Kolpez Kolpe
2003
Documentation table; Dimensions variable
Courtesy of the artist

pp. 178–179
Asier Mendizabal
Face Value
2013
Offset print, wood, glass; 110 × 80 cm
Courtesy of the artist

pp. 180
Katarina Zdjelar
A Girl, the Sun, and an Airplane Airplane
2007
Video, 9 min 50 s
Courtesy of the artist

p. 184
Lise Harlev
My Own Country
2005
2 offset prints on paper; Each 59.4 × 84 cm
Courtesy of the artist

EUROPE^n CLOUD

p. 186–187, 188–189
Tristan Schulze
Europe^n cloud
2012/13
Screen Shots

BEIJING / TAIPEI

p. 205
Oliver Klimpel
Poster
2011

UNE SEMAINE DE BONTÉ (A WEEK OF
KINDNESS)

pp. 13, 74, 78, 100, 162, 190
Especially for this book, Oliver Klimpel and
Aurelia Markwalder have produced a work,
which references Une Semaine de Bonté
(A Week of Kindness), a collage book by the
artist Max Ernst, which was first published in
1934. Ernst's book is devided into seven parts;
the 182 collages from old catalogue and pulp
novel illustrations appeared first as a series of
five pamphlets.

pp. 26, 44, 58, 80, 92, 102, 126, 136, 172
Relating this publication to another sequence
of events, and yet another book, Klimpel and
Markwalder have designed a mimmicking title
typography for each chapter of The Europe^n-
Book and intersecting pages that intertwine
these series of images.

By courtesy of VG BILDKUNST e.V. Bonn
2013

Europe (to the power of) n
was realised within the framework of the Excellence
Initiative of the Goethe-Institut in collaboration with
the Goethe-Institut in Munich and the Regional
Goethe-Institutes in Central and East Europe,
South-East Europe, North-West and South-West
Europe, and East Europe / Central Asia, in Belgrade,
Brussels, İstanbul, Warsaw, London, Minsk, Vilnius,
Oslo, Beijing, and Madrid.

Organiser is
the Goethe-Institut London.

Co-Organisers are
Curating Contemporary Art Programme /
Royal College of Art, London; Muzeum Sztuki, Łódź;
Henie-Onstad Kunstsenter, Høvikodden / Oslo;
Office for European Capital of Culture 2016, Donostia –
San Sebastián.

Associated Partners are
Contemporary Art Study Centre / European Humanities
University, Vilnius; Novaja Europa Magazine, Minsk;
Galerie Ў, Minsk; SALT, İstanbul; Muzej savremene
umetnosti Vojvodine, Novi Sad; Sint-Lukasgalerie,
Brussels; San Telmo Museoa, Donostia – San Sebastián;
Taipei Contemporary Art Centre, Taipei; Vitamin
Creative Space, Beijing.

Europe (to the power of) n was supported by the
Goethe-Institut, the Cultural Programme of the
European Union, the Robert Bosch Foundation, and the
Allianz Cultural Foundation.

This project has been funded with support from the
European Commission. This publication reflects
the views only of the authors, and the Commission
cannot be held responsible for any use which may be
made of the information contained therein.

With the support of the Culture Programme of the European Union

Partner Institutions are

Royal College of Art
Postgraduate Art and Design

галерэя
сучаснага мастацтва

European Humanities University

Muzeum Sztuki

HOSTED BY SALT

HENIE ONSTAD
KUNSTSENTER

MUSEUM OF CONTEMPORARY ART VOJVODINA

SLG
Sint-Lukasgalerie

STM
San Telmo Museoa

DONOSTIA 2016
SAN SEBASTIAN

Vitamin Creative Space

Taipei Contemporary Art Center
台北當代藝術中心

Locally Supported by

Haus der Kulturen der Welt

Новая Еўропа

CASC

CENTER FOR GERMAN STUDIES

NDG

CAPITALE EUROPEA DELLA CULTURA

European Economic and Social Committee

EUROPEAN UNION
Committee of the Regions

Wilgelover

swiss arts council
prohelvetia

iaspis
The Swedish Arts Grants Committee's International Programme for Visual Artists

LEILA HELLER GALLERY.

DEWEER GALLERY

Donostiako Udala
Ayuntamiento de San Sebastián

今藝術
ARTCO

Bindwerk

Special Thanks to

Jane Alexander, Maryia Aukhimovich, Sylvia Binger, Jacqueline Cabaço, Meiya Cheng, Kirsten Einfeldt, Lara Fresko, Leila Haghighat, Milena Høgsberg, Mona Kriegler, Luka Kulić, Luise Marbach, Markus Müller, Mark Nash, Ruth Noack, Sonia Nieśpiałowska-Owczarek, Igor Otxoa Odriozola, Jane Pavitt, Christian Rudolph, Iñigo Egizabal Ruiz, Dietmar Sattler, Bernd M. Scherer, Stephan Schikora, Luise Schröder, Siv M. Skorpen Brekke, Olga Shparaga, Irina Solomatina, Philipp Sperrle, Po Chi Su, Jarosław Suchan, Sarina Sweenie, Inez Templeton, Gunhild Varvin, Jochen Visscher, Victoria Walsh, Monika Wesołowska, Natalia Zemchionok

Translations by
Deborah Ann Arnfinsen, Louise Bromby,
Žarko Cvejić, Jennifer Calleja, Marcin Wawrzyńczak

Proofreading by
Vanessa Boni, Christopher Köhler, Inez Templeton

Image Processing, Printing, and Binding by
DZA Druckerei zu Altenburg GmbH

Published by
jovis Verlag GmbH
Kurfürstenstraße 15 / 16
10785 Berlin
www.jovis.de

jovis books are available worldwide in selected bookstores. Please contact your nearest bookseller or visit
www.jovis.de for information concerning your local distribution.

Bibliographic information published by the Deutsche Nationalbibliothek
The Deutsche Nationalbibliothek lists this publication in the Deutsche Nationalbibliografie;
detailed bibliographic data are available on the Internet at http://dnb.d-nb.de

This book was edited by
Barbara Steiner on behalf of the Goethe-Institut

Book concept by
Oliver Klimpel and Barbara Steiner

Designed by
Oliver Klimpel, Aurelia Markwalder, and
Leila Tabassomi

Texts by
Peio Aguirre, Frank Baumann, Georg Blochmann,
Christine Bock, Johannes Ebert, Lara Fresko,
Ellen Marie Fodstad, Berthold Franke,
Claudia Hahn-Raabe, Kit Hammonds, Tone Hansen,
Margareta Hauschild, Sabine Hentzsch, Johanna M. Keller,
Oliver Klimpel, Christopher Köhler, Ilina Koralova,
Jarosław Lubiak / Joanna Sokołowska, Filip Luyckx,
Matthias Müller-Wieferig, Lena Prents,
Esra Sarigedik Öktem, Barbara Steiner, Miško Šuvaković,
Christian Teckert, Florian Wüst, Jun Yang,
Kristiane Zappel

ISBN 978-3-86859-250-4